Life-Study
of
1 & 2 Chronicles
Ezra
Nehemiah
Esther

Witness Lee

Living Stream Ministry
Anaheim, California

First Edition, June 1995.

ISBN 978-0-87083-873-6

Published by

Living Stream Ministry
2431 W. La Palma Ave., Anaheim, CA 92801 U.S.A.
P. O. Box 2121, Anaheim, CA 92814 U.S.A.

Printed in the United States of America

11   12   13   14   15   /   12   11   10   9   8   7   6   5

First and Second Chronicles

CONTENTS

v

MESSAGE SIX   THE SUPPLEMENT   **PAGE 37**
TO THE HISTORY OF
THE KINGS OF JUDAH   (1)

Ezra

CONTENTS

Nehemiah

CONTENTS

THE NATURAL VIRTUES AND CAPACITIES BEING BROUGHT TO
THE CROSS IN ORDER TO BE BROUGHT INTO RESURRECTION
(12)

The Example of Moses — The Example of Peter — Entering into Resurrection — An Important Principle

NEHEMIAH'S LIVING IN RESURRECTION   (15)

III. THE RECONSTITUTION OF THE NATION OF GOD'S ELECT   (17)

    A. Coming Back to God by Coming Back to His Law, His Word —
B. Making a Clear Confession to God of Their Past and Making a Firm
Covenant with God

    C. The Arrangement of the Dwelling Place of the People and the
Appointment of the Officers of the Levitical Service and of the Civil Affairs
— D. A Record of the Priests and Levites — E. The Dedication of the
Rebuilt Wall — F. The Appointment of the Services of the Priests and the
Levites and the Supply of Their Needs — G. The Clearance Exercised on
Israel as God's Elect — H. Appointing Duties for the Priests and the
Levites, for the Wood Offering, and for the Firstfruits

NEHEMIAH'S PARTICULAR CHARACTERISTICS   (29)

Being a Pleasant Person with a Proper Attitude and Behavior —
A Person Who Loved God and God's Interest on Earth — One Who
Prayed to Contact God in Fellowship — A Person Who Trusted in God
and Who Was One with God — Altogether Unselfish — Not Indulging in
Lust

NEHEMIAH GOING TO EZRA FOR HELP IN RECONSTITUTING
THE NATION OF GOD'S ELECT   (32)

RE-EDUCATION FOR RECONSTITUTION   (32)

THE RETURNED ISRAELITES BECOMING GOD'S TESTIMONY
(32)

Esther

CONTENTS

THE ESCHATOLOGY
OF THE CHURCH
ACCORDING TO
THE DIVINE REVELATION
OF THE SCRIPTURES

LIFE-STUDY OF FIRST
AND SECOND CHRONICLES

MESSAGE ONE

AN INTRODUCTORY WORD

Scripture Reading: 1 Chron. 1:1-27

There are twelve historical books in the Old Testament. The first three are Joshua, Judges, and Ruth, and the last three are Ezra, Nehemiah, and Esther. In between these two groups of three books, there are three pairs of books: 1 and 2 Samuel, 1 and 2 Kings, and 1 and 2 Chronicles. With this message we begin the life-study of 1 and 2 Chronicles, Ezra, Nehemiah, and Esther. The burden of the life-study of these books can be expressed in the following four statements:

1. In the eternal economy of God, the Father has allotted the Son, the all-inclusive Christ typified by the good land, to the believers as their eternal portion and has transferred them into Him that they may partake of Him (Col. 1:12; 1 Cor. 1:30, 9).

2. The enjoyment of Christ differs in degrees according to the believers' pursuing of Christ and their faithfulness to Him, and the highest attainment of pursuing Christ is to reign with Christ in His divine life through His abounding grace (Phil. 3:13-14; Rom. 5:17b, 21b).

3. The captivity of the believers by the enemy is the top failure of the believers in the enjoyment of Christ by not knowing the power of Christ's resurrection nor living by the bountiful supply of the Spirit of Jesus Christ (Phil. 3:10; 1:19b).

4. The omnipresent and omnipotent Triune God became the hiding God in taking care of His chosen people in the dispersion of their captivity, in the most wise secrecy of His highest sovereignty (Esth. 1—10).

The Bible actually tells us only one thing—God's eternal economy according to the good pleasure of His heart's desire. Our God is exceedingly great, and surely He must have a good pleasure. Based upon His good pleasure He made an eternal economy. The reality, the center, and the goal of God's economy is the all-inclusive and excellent Christ. The entire Bible is for this one thing, not for anything else.

The Bible is arranged in two sections. The first section, the Old Testament, is the section of pictures. God is surely the best writer, and He uses pictures in the first thirty-nine books of His writing in the Bible. These books are therefore full of pictures accompanied by prophecies. The pictures are the types, figures, and shadows in the Old Testament. For instance, Adam is "a type of Him who was to come" (Rom. 5:14). Some types are also prophecies. These prophecies are not in plain words but in pictures. The greatest type in the Old Testament is the history of the people of Israel, who typify God's people on earth today. Thus, the history of Israel in the Old Testament is a big type signifying things to come.

When we come to the twelve books of history in the Old Testament, we should not be distracted by the history presented in these books. Why, then, should we pay attention to the books of history? To answer this question we need to realize that the entire Bible is for God's economy with Christ as the reality, the center, and the goal. In our reading of the books of history, we need to pray and seek the proper interpretation of all the types and prophecies in these books. In particular, we need to find and know the intrinsic significance of all the types. We should focus our attention on the center of these types, which is Christ as the center of God's economy. Therefore, as we are seeking to know the intrinsic significance of what is recorded in the books of history in the Old Testament, we must endeavor to link the history books to God's economy. This is what we are doing in this life-study.

I. FIRST AND SECOND CHRONICLES
BEING ONE BOOK IN THE HEBREW SCRIPTURES

In the Hebrew Scriptures, 1 and 2 Chronicles were one book.

II. THE WRITER

The writer of 1 and 2 Chronicles was probably Ezra. Regarding this matter, we should compare 2 Chronicles 36:22-23 with Ezra 1:1-3a. The repetition in these two portions might be a proof that 1 and 2 Chronicles were written by Ezra, the writer of the book of Ezra.

III. THE TIME

The first book covers about 41 years, from 1056 to 1015 B.C., not including the forefathers' genealogy. The second book covers about 479 years, from 1015 to 536 B.C.

IV. THE PLACE

These two books might have been written in Jerusalem after Ezra's coming back from the captivity.

V. THE CONTENT

The books of 1 and 2 Chronicles cover the genealogy of mankind from Adam to Abraham and the genealogy of God's elect from Abraham to the family of Saul, and the history of Israel from Saul the king to Israel's return from their captivity. From this we see that 1 and 2 Chronicles cover three kinds of history: the history from Adam to Abraham, which concerns the whole world; the history from Abraham to Saul, which concerns the forefathers of the race of Israel, before they were formed into a nation; and the history of the kingdom of Israel, from the time of Saul to the coming back from their captivity.

VI. THE CENTRAL THOUGHT

The matter of the central thought of 1 and 2 Chronicles is very crucial.

A. To Give a Full Chronology of God's Move in Man's History

The central thought is, first, to give us a full chronology of God's move in man's history by including the genealogy from Adam to Samuel, indicating that God's move in man's history to prepare the way for God to carry out His eternal economy in humanity by becoming a man that man may become God is not a matter that concerns only the history of God's elect but a matter that concerns the history of the entire race of mankind. The central point of view in 1 and 2 Samuel and 1 and 2 Kings is the chosen people of God, but in 1 and 2 Chronicles it is the entire race of mankind. This needs a lineage not from Samuel but from Adam to Christ, which corresponds to the genealogy of Christ as recorded in Luke 3, not as presented in Matthew 1. The view in Matthew 1 is narrow and is limited to Israel. The view in Luke 3 is broad and includes all of mankind. This is a strong evidence that the coming Christ as the embodiment of God is not only for the one race chosen by God but for the entire human race created by God.

We need to see that God's move is in man's history. Have you ever heard such a phrase as "God's move in man's history"? Do you believe that in today's tumultuous world situation God is still moving in man's history? We need to believe that God has been moving and is still moving in and through man's history. In Adam's history God moved, and in Abel's history God also moved. This was a move on the positive side. But God moved even in Cain's history. This was a move on the negative side.

I can testify from my observation of the world situation since 1918 and from my study of the prophecies in the Bible that God surely moves in man's history. Let us consider, for example, the dispute over Palestine, that is, over the good land, that has been going on for hundreds of years. Who is the landlord, the rightful owner, of the good land—Israel or the Arabs? The Jews say that Palestine is the land of their forefathers, and the Arabs claim that it is the land of their forefathers. This issue has not been settled but is still on the negotiating table. The statesmen involved in these negotiations are foolish men, for they do not know God or the Word of God, the Bible, yet they are talking about God's affairs. God is the landlord of Palestine, and only He can solve the problem concerning this land. I believe that while the statesmen are negotiating over the ownership of the good land, the Lord is in the heavens laughing (Psa. 2:4). The decision regarding the good land will not be made by statesmen; it will be made by the One who is in the heavens. Soon the Lord Jesus may come back and settle this matter. When He comes He may say to the statesmen of the world, "This is not your business—it is My business."

We have pointed out that the chronology in 1 and 2 Chronicles indicates that God's move in man's history is to prepare the way for God to carry out His eternal economy in humanity by becoming a man that man may become God. If this cannot be accomplished, there is no way to solve the problems of today's world situation. All the problems on this earth are waiting for one thing—for a good number of men to become God-men. This matter concerns not only the history of God's elect, Israel, but also the history of the entire race of mankind.

The world situation has changed greatly during the past fifty years. In these fifty years God has blended together people from everywhere on earth. In our semi-annual trainings saints come together from fifty nations. This would have been impossible fifty years ago. This blending of the nations is something that could have been accomplished only by God.

Through such a blending thousands of God-men will be produced. In Russia, for instance, the God-men are spreading and increasing. The whole world is open to the ministry in the Lord's recovery. This ministry has reached to all six continents, and I have received letters of appreciation from saints in many different countries saying that they are open to receive this ministry.

Recently I released the matter of the high peak of God's revelation—the revelation that God became a man so that man may become God in life and in nature (but not in the Godhead) for the producing of the Body of Christ as His expression. Now we need to pray that the Lord will give us a new revival, a revival which has never been seen in man's history. Such a revival will be something new, for it is related to God's "hobby," to His good pleasure, to the desire of His heart. God's good pleasure is that God would become a man to make man God in life and in nature. This is the desire of God's heart, the "hobby" in His heart, and He will accomplish it.

As we have seen, whereas the central point of view in 1 and 2 Samuel and in 1 and 2 Kings is the chosen race of God, the central point of view in 1 and 2 Chronicles is the entire race of mankind. This indicates that God thinks not only about Israel but also about the Gentiles. Most of us are not of the people of Israel, but God thought about us in eternity past. Ephesians 1:4 tells us we all were chosen by God before the foundation of the world. We praise the Lord for choosing us in Christ before the foundation of the world.

B. To Present Some Important Details of God's Dealing with the Kings of Judah

The central thought of 1 and 2 Chronicles is also to present to us some of the important details of God's dealing with the kings of Judah that are not recorded in 1 and 2 Samuel and in 1 and 2 Kings. Many readers of the Bible feel that 1 and 2 Chronicles are somewhat repetitious, covering things which have been covered already in 1 and 2 Samuel and in 1 and 2 Kings. We need to see that at the beginning of 1 Chronicles a part of mankind's history is recorded that is recorded neither in 1 and 2 Samuel nor in 1 and 2 Kings. Furthermore, at the end of 1 Chronicles there is a supplement to David's history, and in 2 Chronicles there is a supplement to the history of the kings of Judah. Israel was divided into two nations: the northern kingdom, called the kingdom of Israel, and the southern kingdom, called the kingdom of Judah. The good kings were not in Israel but in Judah. Second Chronicles does not touch the kings of Israel but covers only the kings of Judah, giving us details not found elsewhere concerning God's dealing with them and also telling us the reasons why God dealt with them in the way He did.

C. To Give a Complete History of God's Move in Man's History

Finally, in 1 and 2 Chronicles we have a complete history of God's move in man's history from Adam to Abraham, from

Abraham to Samuel, and from Samuel, who brought in the kingship, to Israel's return from their captivity.

VII. THE SECTIONS
OF THE COVERAGE OF THE PRESENT STUDY

In this life-study we will not cover all of 1 and 2 Chronicles but only certain parts of these books. Mainly we will cover those parts of 1 and 2 Chronicles that are a supplement to the history in 1 and 2 Kings. The matters covered in the life-study of 1 and 2 Samuel and in the life-study of 1 and 2 Kings will not be repeated here.

The sections of the coverage of our present study include the genealogy from Adam to the twelve tribes of Israel (1 Chron. 1—9); the supplement to the history of David (1 Chron. 22:2—29:30); and the supplement to the history of the kings of Judah (2 Chron. 11:5-23; 13:1-21; 14:6—15:15; 17:1-19; 19:1—20:30; 21:12-18; 24:14b-24; 25:5-16; 26:6-21a; 28:8-15; 29:3—32:8; 33:11-17; 34:3-7; 36:20b-23). Therefore, this study will cover three things: the genealogy of mankind, the supplement to the history of David, and the supplement to the history of the kings of Judah.

LIFE-STUDY OF FIRST
AND SECOND CHRONICLES

THE REPRODUCTION OF GOD

Scripture Reading: Gen. 1:26; 3:15; 22:18; 2 Sam. 7:12-14; John 12:24

In this message I have the burden to speak a word on a very striking matter—the reproduction of God.

MAN CREATED
ACCORDING TO GOD'S KIND

After God created the heavens and the earth, one of the angels rebelled and became God's enemy, Satan. This ruined God's original creation. Eventually, God came in to repair, remodel, and restore the universe. In this restoration God created billions of living creatures, including all kinds of birds and animals. Although God created so many living creatures, not one of these creatures was like Him. So God made man in His image and according to His likeness (Gen. 1:26). Therefore, man was not created according to his own kind but according to God's kind. God did not create mankind; He created man according to God's kind.

After God finished the creation of Adam and his wife, He looked upon everything that He had made. As He looked upon the earth and everything in it, only Adam and Eve were His delight, His "hobby." Only they could make God happy because only they were His kind. When God looked at Adam, He might have said, "I am pleased to see man. This is My hobby; this is My kind." However, God's hobby was far from complete because at that time man had only God's image and God's likeness but not God's life and God's nature. Man had God's image, but he did not have God Himself.

GOD BECOMING A MAN

According to His eternal plan God Himself had to become a man. God is almighty and omnipotent, but He never does things in a fast way. We may have an idea and then act upon it immediately. God is not like this. He is very slow and full of patience. He made an economy in eternity past. Then He created the heavens and the earth. Later He repaired and restored the ruined creation, and as the last work in His restoration and further creation, God created man, His hobby. Yet that was not God's real hobby. God's real hobby is that God Himself would become a man.

After Adam's fall and after promising Eve that He would come as the seed of the woman (Gen. 3:15), God waited thousands of years before becoming a man. If I had been His companion, I would have said, "God, since the desire of Your heart is that You become a man, why would You not do this right now? You told the fallen man that You would come as the seed of the woman. Why would You not come as this seed today?" If God had been asked such questions, He might have said, "I am not small like you are. I am great, and with Me a thousand years are as one day."

Approximately two thousand years after making the promise in Genesis 3:15, God promised Abraham a seed that would be a blessing to all the nations (22:18). God seemed to be saying, "Abraham, you will have a seed. This seed will be I Myself becoming a man to be the blessing to all the earth." Unable to be patient, Abraham followed Sarah's suggestion that he have a child by her handmaid, Hagar. Instead of producing the promised seed, Abraham produced a wrong one, Ishmael. God, however, continued to wait before becoming a man.

After another thousand years, up to David's time, God still had not come as a man. But God told David that he would have a seed who would be God's Son (2 Sam. 7:12-14). This Son is just God Himself. God prophesied to David concerning this seed, but He still did not come as a man.

Eventually, after another one thousand years, four thousand years after the creation of Adam, God came to be a man, conceived of the Holy Spirit and born of a human virgin

(Matt. 1:20, 23). He grew up for thirty more years, but no one knew that He was God become a man, a God-man.

THE ONE GRAIN PRODUCING MANY GRAINS

One day the Lord Jesus, the God-man, said that He was a grain of wheat falling into the ground to die in order to become many grains (John 12:24). These many grains are actually many gods as the reproduction of God. The first grain—the first God-man—was a prototype, and the many grains—the many God-men—produced by this one grain through death and resurrection are the mass reproduction. This is the reproduction of God. When some hear that God has been reproduced, they may be shocked and say that such a word is nonsensical. Nevertheless, this is what is revealed in John 12:24.

God's real hobby is to have His reproduction in many nations around the globe. Such a reproduction makes God happy because His reproduction looks like Him, speaks like Him, and lives like Him. God is in this reproduction, and His reproduction has His life, His nature, and His constitution. What a great matter this is!

GOD DOING THE WORK OF TRANSFORMATION WITH PATIENCE

Although we are God's reproduction, this reproduction—God's hobby—is not so complete or perfect, because many of us who have God's life do not live by His life. Some do live by God's life, but they do not live by His life continually. Perhaps in the morning they live by God's life, but later in the day they may lose their temper and live like a scorpion. This means that in the morning they are gods, but later they are "scorpions." In the evening they may become even worse, living like the devil, Satan. It is not too much to say that a believer in Christ can live like Satan. One day the Lord Jesus turned to Peter, someone who loved Him, and said to him, "Get behind Me, Satan!" (Matt. 16:23a). Because Peter had become Satan, he needed to bear his cross so that Satan could be put on the cross.

In our daily living we may be God at one time, a scorpion at another time, and Satan at yet another time. Because this is our actual situation, we surely need to be transformed. Do you know what our God is doing today? God is doing the work of transformation in us with patience.

REVOLUTIONIZED BY REALIZING WHO WE ARE

Since the ministry began in the United States in 1962, I have actually ministered only one matter—God becoming a man that man may become God in life and in nature. However, it was not until February 1994 that I received such a clear view with a heavy burden to tell God's people that we all are God in life and in nature but not in the Godhead.

To know who we are and to realize who we are revolutionizes us. Suppose a certain brother who has been living like a scorpion realizes that, as a child of God, he is God in life and in nature. Immediately this brother will be radically changed. The atmosphere and everything related to him will also be changed. If all of today's Christians realized that they were God in life and in nature, the whole world would be different.

During the past ten months, I have often checked with myself: "Is a God-man like this? You have spoken that the believers have become God in life and in nature, yet what are you now? Are you God or are you something else?" My answer has been to repent and ask for the Lord's forgiveness because at least some of the things I did were not in Him or according to Him. This realization has revolutionized me.

THE STALENESS OF FUNDAMENTAL CHRISTIANITY

On the one hand, outwardly God as the Ruler of the universe has done many things so that people from everywhere in the world can be blended. On the other hand, God has a recovery on earth, and His recovery has been under His leading for seventy-two years. During these years He has released thousands of printed messages, and these messages are in thousands of homes. These messages have been received in many countries around the world. On a regular basis I receive letters of appreciation. Recently someone wrote to me saying that he had been listening to lies about us, but when he read the *Life-study of Galatians,* his eyes were opened and he could see the truth. Such publications have reached many nations, and we believe that the Lord will use them to gain what He desires.

Christianity has been on earth for more than nineteen centuries. It has kept and continues to teach the fundamental faith. But its fundamental faith has not reached the peak of the divine revelation—that God became a man through incarnation and then passed through human living, death, and resurrection in order to have a mass reproduction of Himself. Because fundamental Christianity has not reached this peak, the fundamental teachings have become stale. As a result, many in the denominations do not have a goal, and they do not know where they should go. Even many leading ones in today's Christianity do not know how to go on; they have nowhere to go. Visit the Christian bookstores and see what kind of books are being sold there. Many books are filled with old, stale fundamental teachings.

Because fundamental Christianity has become stale, it has lost its impact and effect, like salt which has become tasteless (Matt. 5:13). Who is the salt among the Christians in the United States? Salt is supposed to kill corruption, but where is this killing power among today's Christians? In most communities it is hard to tell who are Christians and who are not Christians. All the people are about the same.

THE HIGH PEAK OF THE DIVINE REVELATION

I am glad that during the last ten months the Lord has released the matter of the high peak of the divine revelation in the Holy Scriptures. Recently, I wrote in Chinese a hymn on God becoming a man that man may become God in life and in nature. Many saints are beside themselves with joy when they sing this hymn. It is very difficult to translate this hymn into English. The following is a literal translation:

1 How great a miracle! How deep a mystery!
   God and man are joined and blended as one!
   God becomes man and man becomes God,
   An economy incomprehensible to angels and
     mankind;

Out of God's pleasure, in His love,
Attaining the highest purpose of God.

2 God incarnated to be a God-man,
In order that I may become God,
In life and nature the same kind as He,
Having no share in His Godhead;
His attributes become my virtues,
His glorious image livingly expressed through me.

3 It is no longer I living alone,
But God and I living together;
Coordinated with the saints in God
To be built up as the universal house
    of the Divine Trinity
And to become the organic Body of Christ
As a great corporate vessel for Him to
    express Himself.

4 Ultimately, the holy city, Jerusalem,
The aggregate of visions and revelations,
The Triune God and the tripartite man
To be the couple in love in eternity
    as man yet God;
The mutual habitation of divinity and humanity
With God's glory shining forth radiantly in man.

The following is a translation of this hymn in poetry to the
tune of #499 in *Hymns:*

1 What miracle! What mystery!
That God and man should blended be!
God became man to make man God,
Untraceable economy!
From His good pleasure, heart's desire,
His highest goal attained will be.

2 Flesh He became, the first God-man,
His pleasure that I God may be:
In life and nature I'm God's kind,
Though Godhead's His exclusively.
His attributes my virtues are;
His glorious image shines through me.

3 No longer I alone that live,
But God together lives with me.
Built with the saints in the Triune God,
His universal house we'll be,
And His organic Body we
For His expression corp'rately.

4 Jerusalem, the ultimate,
Of visions the totality;
The Triune God, tripartite man—
A loving pair eternally—
As man yet God they coinhere,
A mutual dwelling place to be;
God's glory in humanity
Shines forth in splendor radiantly!

According to this hymn, it is a great miracle and a deep mystery that God has a way to be joined to man and mingled with man. God became man that man may become God. Such an economy is incomprehensible to both angels and man. This economy is of God's desire, and it will reach, attain, the high peak of God's goal. Ultimately the holy city, Jerusalem, will be the aggregate of all the visions and revelations throughout the Scriptures. The Triune God and the tripartite man will become a loving couple in eternity as man yet still God. Divinity and humanity will become a mutual abode, and the glory of God will be expressed in humanity radiantly in splendor to the uttermost.

I hope that the saints in all the churches throughout the earth, especially the co-workers and the elders, will see this revelation and then rise up to pray that God would give us a new revival—a revival which has never been recorded in history.

LIFE-STUDY OF FIRST
AND SECOND CHRONICLES

MESSAGE THREE

THE GENEALOGY FROM ADAM
TO THE TWELVE TRIBES OF ISRAEL

Scripture Reading: 1 Chron. 1—9

In this message we will consider the genealogy from Adam to the twelve tribes of Israel. This genealogy is covered in the first nine chapters of 1 Chronicles.

I. THE GENEALOGY FROM ADAM TO ABRAHAM

In 1:1-27 we have the genealogy from Adam to Abraham. The main characters in this genealogy are Adam, Enosh, Enoch, and Noah.

II. THE GENEALOGY OF ABRAHAM

Verses 28 through 34 speak of the genealogy of Abraham. The main characters here are Abraham, Isaac, and Israel.

III. THE GENEALOGY OF ESAU

The genealogy of Esau (vv. 35-54) is not in the lineage of the genealogy of Christ as recorded in Matthew 1:1-17 and Luke 3:23-38.

IV. THE GENEALOGY OF ISRAEL

Chapters two through nine are a record of the genealogy of Israel. Israel had twelve sons. All the twelve sons became the fathers of the twelve tribes. The following chapters through chapter nine are the genealogies of these twelve tribes.

V. THE GENEALOGY OF JUDAH

First Chronicles 2:3—4:23 is the genealogy of Judah.

A. The Main Characters

The main characters in this genealogy are Judah, Caleb, Boaz, Jesse, David, and Solomon.

B. The Tribe of Judah Being the Royal Tribe

The tribe of Judah is the royal tribe (5:2a), producing kings from David to Christ. Hence, the genealogy of Judah, among the twelve genealogies of the twelve tribes, is the only one that is counted as the lineage of the genealogy of Christ as recorded in Matthew 1 and Luke 3.

C. The Striking Matter in Judah's Genealogy

In Judah's genealogy the striking matter is that Judah begot Pherez of his daughter-in-law Tamar (2:4). The Bible is honest in recording this matter.

D. A Particular Prayer by One of the Descendants of Judah

In 4:10 we have a particular prayer offered by one of the descendants of Judah: "Jabez called on the God of Israel saying, Oh that You would richly bless me and enlarge my border, and that Your hand would be with me, and that You would so keep me from evil that it would not grieve me!" God caused what Jabez had requested to come to pass. I hope that all of us would have such a prayer, a prayer that God would enlarge the border of the enjoyment of the good land; that is, enlarge the border of our enjoyment of Christ. We all need to pray, "O God, enlarge my border in the gaining of Christ and in the enjoyment of Christ."

E. Matters Included in the Genealogy of Judah

The genealogy of Judah includes the genealogy of David and the genealogy of Solomon.

1. The Genealogy of David

The genealogy of David is recorded in 3:1-9. David had six sons born during his reign in Hebron for seven and a half years. Thirteen sons of David were born during his reign in

Jerusalem for thirty-three years, including Solomon, born of
Bath-shua (Bath-sheba). In addition, David had a daughter,
Tamar, and also sons born of his concubines.

2. The Genealogy of Solomon

The main characters in the genealogy of Solomon (vv. 10-24)
are Solomon, Asa, Hezekiah, and Zerubbabel.

VI. THE GENEALOGY OF SIMEON

The genealogy of Simeon is recorded in 4:24-43. The
remarkable thing concerning this tribe is that they had rich
and good pasture, spacious, quiet, and peaceful, and that they
defeated the Amalekites. We today should also have such a
rich and spacious pasture. This means that our enjoyment of
Christ as our good land should be spacious, quiet, and
peaceful.

VII. THE GENEALOGY OF REUBEN

Next we have the genealogy of Reuben (5:1-10). Reuben
was the firstborn son of Israel. Because he defiled his father's
bed, his birthright was given to the two sons of Joseph for
the inheritance of the double portion of the good land as the
two tribes (vv. 1-2). This should be a warning to us that the
birthright of enjoying Christ can be lost because of our
failure.

VIII. THE GENEALOGY OF GAD

The genealogy of Gad is recorded in verses 11 through 17.

IX. AN INSERTION

Verses 18 through 26 are an insertion.

A. The Children of Reuben, the Gadites,
and Half the Tribe of Manasseh Defeating
Their Enemies and Possessing Their Land

The children of Reuben, the Gadites, and half the tribe
of Manasseh defeated their enemies and possessed their land
by the help of God, for they cried out to God in the battle
and trusted in Him (vv. 18-23). This is a good example for us

today. We should cry out to God, telling Him that we want to gain more of Christ, possess more of Christ, and enjoy more of Christ.

B. The Children of Reuben, the Gadites, and Half the Tribe of Manasseh Trespassing against God

The children of Reuben, the Gadites, and half the tribe of Manasseh trespassed against God and went as harlots after the gods of the peoples of Canaan. Then the God of Israel stirred up the kings of Assyria to come to capture them and bring them away from their land (vv. 25-26).

X. THE GENEALOGY OF LEVI

In chapter six we have the genealogy of Levi, the priestly tribe.

A. One of the Sons of Levi Being Kohath

One of the sons of Levi was Kohath, one of the sons of Kohath was Amram, and Amram's sons were Aaron and Moses, and his daughter was Miriam (vv. 1-3). This is the genealogy of Aaron, Moses, and Miriam.

B. A Descendant of Aaron Being Captured to Babylon

A descendant of Aaron, Jehozadak, was captured to Babylon by Nebuchadnezzar (v. 15). It was most unfortunate that even a descendant of the priestly tribe was taken away into captivity in Babylon.

C. The Prophet Samuel Being a Descendant of the Great Rebel Korah

The prophet Samuel was a descendant of the great rebel Korah, who was a descendant of Kohath, the son of Levi (vv. 16-27); and the grandson of Samuel, Heman, was a singer in the temple and a psalmist (v. 33; Psa. 88, title). Korah, the forefather, was a great rebel, yet one of his descendants was Samuel and another was Heman. This indicates that God's mercy and grace are unlimited.

D. David Setting the Descendants of Kohath over the Service of Song in the House of Jehovah

After the ark of testimony was given rest by David, David set the descendants of Kohath over the service of song in the house of Jehovah, and they ministered before the tabernacle with singing until Solomon built the temple in Jerusalem. They attended to their office, and their brothers the Levites were given to all the service of the tabernacle of the house of God (1 Chron. 6:31-48). In typology this signifies the church service, in which everything must be set in order by the arrangement of the Spirit.

E. Aaron and His Sons Being the Priests

Aaron and his sons were the priests, dwelling in thirteen cities (vv. 49-60).

F. The Levites Dwelling in Cities among the Tribes

In verses 61 through 81 we are told that the Levites dwelt in the cities among the tribes.

XI. THE GENEALOGY OF ISSACHAR

In 7:1-5 we have the genealogy of Issachar. The families of Issachar were famous in having mighty men of valor. They were excellent warriors.

XII. THE GENEALOGY OF BENJAMIN

The genealogy of Benjamin is found in 7:6-12 and 8:1-40. The main characters are Saul and Jonathan (8:33). The sons of Benjamin were warlike (7:9, 11; 8:40) and dwelt near Jerusalem.

XIII. THE GENEALOGY OF NAPHTALI

First Chronicles 7:13 records the genealogy of Naphtali.

XIV. THE GENEALOGY OF MANASSEH

Verses 14 through 19 are concerned with the genealogy of Manasseh.

XV. THE GENEALOGY OF EPHRAIM

The genealogy of Ephraim is given in verses 20 through 29. The people of Ephraim dwelt around Bethel.

XVI. THE GENEALOGY OF ASHER

In the genealogy of Asher (vv. 30-40), we are told that the tribe of Asher had mighty men of valor and were warlike (v. 40).

XVII. THE GENEALOGY OF THE RETURNED CHILDREN OF ISRAEL

In 9:1-34 we have the genealogy of the returned children of Israel. The first ones who dwelt in their possessions in their cities were the children of Israel, the priests, the Levites, and the Nethinim, who were the servants, or the caretakers, of the temple (v. 2). Those who dwelt in Jerusalem were some of the children of Judah, some of the children of Benjamin, and some of the children of Ephraim and Manasseh (vv. 3-9). The priests (vv. 10-13) and the Levites (vv. 14-34) dwelt in Jerusalem. Among the serving Levites were the descendants of Korah, the great rebel against God and Moses (vv. 19, 31; Num. 16).

XVIII. THE GENEALOGY OF THE HOUSE OF SAUL

Finally, in 1 Chronicles 9:35-44 we have the genealogy of the house of Saul who dwelt in Gibeon.

In this message we have presented simply a general idea of the genealogy from Adam to the twelve tribes of Israel. I believe that if you read these chapters carefully, the Spirit will show you the spiritual significance of the things covered here.

LIFE-STUDY OF FIRST
AND SECOND CHRONICLES

MESSAGE FOUR

THE HIGHEST POINT OF GOD'S GOSPEL

Scripture Reading: 1 Tim. 1:4; Gen. 1:26; John 12:24; 1 Cor. 10:17; Col. 3:11

In this message I have the burden to speak a word on the highest point of God's gospel—God becoming a man that man may become God in life and in nature but not in the Godhead.

GOD'S KIND AND MANKIND

The eternal God in His eternity had a "dream" according to His heart's desire, and He made a plan, which in the New Testament is called God's economy (1 Tim. 1:4; Eph. 1:10; 3:9). Then God created the universe, making His heart's desire (Adam) the center. This heart's desire is nothing less than one who is the same kind as God is (Gen. 1:26), one who would reproduce and fill the whole earth (v. 28).

God made man after His kind. This means that before the fall of man there was no mankind, only God's kind. Contrary to the definitions given in Webster's dictionary, from God's point of view the word *mankind* is a negative term, for there should be no mankind, only the man created by God as God's kind. However, after the fall man separated himself from God and became mankind. Through this fall Satan came in to cause trouble, and the whole world was thrown into confusion.

Out of the confused world of mankind, God chose Abraham, whose descendants became the nation of Israel. The nation of Israel should not be listed with the nations, because it was among the nations but not with the nations. This nation was a separate people, a holy people sanctified unto God. God used His elect Israel as a type to signify that, among fallen mankind, God would have a people to come in the future.

GOD BECOMING A MAN TO PRODUCE GOD-MAN KIND

Two thousand years after Abraham, the choosing God became a man. This God-man, through His death and resurrection, has made a mass reproduction of Himself. He as the one grain became many grains (John 12:24). The many grains are ground into fine flour and blended together to become one loaf (1 Cor. 10:17). The Lord Jesus as the only begotten Son of God was the one grain, and He made us the many grains, His many "twins," His many brothers (Rom. 8:29), to be blended into one loaf, one Body. Among us there is no difference in nationality, race, or social rank (Col. 3:11). We are a new kind, "God-man kind."

Just as there are new words to describe new developments in human culture, so we need new terms and expressions to describe matters in our spiritual culture. *God-man kind* is such an expression. In Christ God and man have become one entity, the God-man. In God's creation there was no mankind; there was only man as God's kind. It was through man's fall that mankind came into existence. Eventually God became a man to have a mass reproduction of Himself and thereby to produce a new kind. This new kind is neither God's kind nor mankind—it is God-man kind. Today as believers in Christ, we are God-man kind; we are God-men.

GOD BLENDING THE NATIONS ON EARTH
THAT WE, THE GOD-MEN,
MAY BE BLENDED INTO ONE BODY

According to our genealogy, we were scattered far away from one another. How could we be blended into one Body? This is now possible because of the great changes that have taken place on earth during the past fifty years. Through the modern means of transportation and communication, people from all over the earth can be blended. In our semi-annual trainings saints come together from as many as fifty nations. The globe today has become a small earth-ball, making it possible for me to speak the holy Word to people from so many different nations.

On the day I was saved I told the Lord that from that time onward I wanted to travel from village to village in China, preaching the Bible and telling people about Jesus Christ. My intention was to speak only to my countrymen. I never dreamed that I would be here in the United States speaking to saints from fifty nations. From this we see that God has blended the earth together so that we may be blended into one Body.

One day, in 1938, I received from a sister in Peking a letter containing two checks. This sister told me that she believed that God would send me to America and that one check was for my trip there and back and the other was for taking care of my family while I was gone. I answered her, saying that I did not have any burden to go to the United States. But she told me that I should keep the checks and that sooner or later the Lord would send me to the United States. Twenty years later I visited this country, and eventually I became a citizen. This was the Lord's doing. Acts 5:31 tells us that in His ascension the Lord Jesus is the Leader and the Savior. He is the Ruler of all the kings of the earth (Rev. 1:5), and I was sent here by Him.

God created the earth and made man according to His kind. Man fell and became mankind. From fallen mankind God chose Abraham to be the father of another people, and then two thousand years later God became a man and lived on earth as a God-man. I am glad that I have become an American, but I am much more glad that I have become a God-man. I am an American by naturalization, but I am a God-man by regeneration.

Do you know what God wants today? We may say that He wants Christians and believers in Christ. Actually, what God wants is not merely Christians or even believers in Christ; He wants a big group of God-men. I believe that our God, who is sitting in the heavens, is happy whenever He looks upon a gathering of God-men, especially a gathering of God-men from fifty nations. In such a gathering everyone has the appearance of a God-man.

At this juncture I would ask you to consider *Hymns,* #203:

1 In the bosom of the Father,
   Ere the ages had begun,
Thou wast in the Father's glory,
   God's unique begotten Son.
When to us the Father gave Thee,
   Thou in person wast the same,
All the fulness of the Father
   In the Spirit to proclaim.

2 By Thy death and resurrection,
   Thou wast made God's firstborn Son;
By Thy life to us imparting,
   Was Thy duplication done.
We, in Thee regenerated,
   Many sons to God became;
Truly as Thy many brethren,
   We are as Thyself the same.

3 Once Thou wast the only grain, Lord,
   Falling to the earth to die,
That thru death and resurrection
   Thou in life may multiply.
We were brought forth in Thy nature
   And the many grains became;
As one loaf we all are blended,
   All Thy fulness to proclaim.

4 We're Thy total reproduction,
   Thy dear Body and Thy Bride,
Thine expression and Thy fulness,
   For Thee ever to abide.
We are Thy continuation,
   Thy life-increase and Thy spread,
Thy full growth and Thy rich surplus,
   One with Thee, our glorious Head.

This hymn says that once Christ, the only begotten Son, was the only grain. Through His death and resurrection He has made us the many grains. As such grains, we are the many sons of God (Heb. 2:10), Christ's many brothers, His many "twins." Now the many grains are blended as one loaf, which is Christ's Body, His reproduction.

THE DEIFICATION OF MAN

In the second to the fifth centuries, the church fathers found three high mysteries in the Bible: (1) the Triune God, the Divine Trinity, the highest mystery; (2) the person of Christ; and (3) the deification of man—that man could become God in life and in nature but not in the Godhead. However, after the fifth century the truth concerning this last mystery was gradually lost. Using the Nicene Creed, today's Christianity affirms the first two mysteries—the mystery of the Divine Trinity and the mystery of Christ's person—but much of Christianity does not see anything about the third mystery—the mystery of God becoming man that man may become God in life and in nature. There is no teaching regarding this among most Christians today. But I feel strongly the Lord is going to recover this truth. As far as the truth is concerned, this may be the last item that the Lord needs to recover.

REVOLUTIONIZED BY REALIZING
THAT WE ARE GOD-MEN

When we think of ourselves as God-men, this thinking, this realization, revolutionizes us in our daily experience. For example, a brother may be unhappy with his wife. But he remembers that he is a God-man, and immediately his attitude is changed. Then he will desire to be a God-man husband.

We need to understand that to be a part of mankind is to be something negative. In God's view *mankind* is a negative term referring to fallen man. As believers in Christ and children of God, we are not mankind—we are God-man kind. To realize this is to be changed, even revolutionized. When we realize that we are God-men, we will say, "Lord, You are the first God-man, and we are the many God-men following You. You lived a human life, not by Your human life but by God's divine life to express Him. His attributes became Your virtues. You were here on this earth dying every day. You were crucified to live. Lord, You are my life today and You are my person. You are just me. I therefore must die. I need to be conformed to Your death. I have to be crucified to die every day to live a God-man's life, a human life yet not by my human life but by the divine life, with Your life and Your nature as my constitution to express You in Your divine attributes, which become my human virtues." This makes us not just a Christian or a believer in Christ but a God-man, one kind with God. This is the highest point of God's gospel.

PREACHING THE TRUTH THAT GOD BECAME A MAN THAT MAN MAY BECOME GOD IN LIFE AND IN NATURE AND LIVING THE LIFE OF A GOD-MAN TO BRING IN A NEW REVIVAL AND TO END THIS AGE

According to this gospel we were fallen, yet Christ died for us. If we believe in Him and receive Him, we will have the eternal life to be the sons of God. Christians today admit that all the believers in Christ are the sons of God or the children of God, but they do not dare admit that the believers in Christ are God. At the end of this age, we are teaching and preaching the truth that God became a man in order to make man God, the same as He is in life and in nature but not in the Godhead. It is a great blessing to hear this truth.

After hearing that God wants a group of God-men, how can you be content to be anything else? What do you want to be? Do you want to be a typical Chinese or a typical American? Do you want to be merely a Christian or a believer in Christ? We should all declare that we want to live the life of a God-man. Eventually, the God-men will be the victors, the overcomers, the Zion within Jerusalem. This will bring in a new revival which has never been seen in history, and this will end this age.

LIFE-STUDY OF FIRST AND SECOND CHRONICLES

MESSAGE FIVE

THE SUPPLEMENT TO THE HISTORY OF DAVID

Scripture Reading: 1 Chron. 22:2—29:30

First Chronicles 22:2—29:30 is a supplement to the history of David.

I. DAVID'S PREPARATION OF THE MATERIALS FOR THE BUILDING OF THE TEMPLE OF GOD IN ABUNDANCE

David's preparation of the materials for the building of the temple of God in abundance typifies Christ's provision for the building of the church of God with His unsearchable riches (22:2-5, 14-16a; 29:2-5a). All the riches provided by Christ are Christ Himself. David was a type of Christ, fighting the battle and gaining the victory. Christ is the unique One who is qualified to provide the materials for the building up of the church of God. The spiritual significances of all the materials provided by David are covered in the life-study of 1 Kings 5—7.

David's preparation in his affliction, in his trials, and in the victory of his fightings typifies Christ's rich provision for the building of the church of God in His trials and victory over Satan with his power of darkness. According to the record of the New Testament, Christ lived a fighting life, fighting mainly against God's enemy Satan. In His victory He prepared all the materials for the building up of the church of God.

II. DAVID'S CHARGE TO SOLOMON

In 1 Chronicles 22:6-13, 16b we have David's charge to Solomon for the building of the temple of God in peace. The father David was a fighter to gain the provisions. The son Solomon was not a fighter but a peaceful king. In peace he enjoyed what was gained and attained through his father's victories.

III. DAVID'S CHARGE TO ALL THE LEADERS OF ISRAEL

In verses 17 through 19 David charged all the leaders of Israel to help Solomon in building the temple of God.

IV. DAVID'S ARRANGEMENT OF THE ORDER OF THE SERVICES OF THE PRIESTS AND THE LEVITES

Chapters twenty-three through twenty-six are a record of David's arrangement of the order of the services of the priests and the Levites. This typifies that as the Head of the Body Christ has set up an order in His Body for all the members to keep. We need to realize that there is an order in the Body of Christ, with the various members set in a particular place. The arrangement in the Body is not a matter of who is higher and who is lower; rather, the arrangement is altogether a matter of what has been ordered by Christ. We need to realize that all the members of the Body are necessary and useful, and we should be content with where Christ has placed us in His Body.

A. Making Solomon His Son King over Israel

David made Solomon his son the king over Israel, indicating that all the priests and Levites were under him (23:1).

B. The Priests Being Ordered in Twenty-four Divisions

The priests, the sons of Aaron, were ordered in twenty-four divisions, or sections (24:1-19). In the church life today we serve in different sections.

C. The Divisions of the Services of the Levites

David also arranged the divisions of the services of the Levites (23:2-32; 24:20—26:32).

1. The Services of the Descendants
of the Three Sons of Levi

The services of the descendants of the three sons of Levi—
Gershon, Kohath, and Merari—are described in 23:2-23. The
total number of the Levites was thirty-eight thousand males
from thirty years old and upward (vv. 2-3). Of these,
twenty-four thousand were to oversee the work of the house
of Jehovah; six thousand were to be officers and judges; four
thousand were to be gatekeepers; and four thousand were to
praise Jehovah with the instruments made by David (vv. 4-5).
The genealogies of Gershon, Kohath, and Merari are given in
verses 6 through 23.

2. All the Serving Levites
Serving alongside the Priests

All the serving Levites from twenty years old and upward
were to serve alongside the priests to take care of all the
business affairs for the temple of God (vv. 24-32). In today's
church life some of the younger ones should bear some service
for the older ones.

3. The Rest of the Levites
Casting Lots for Their Duty

The rest of the Levites, both old and young, cast lots for
their duty even as their brothers the sons of Aaron (24:20-31).
This is a further indication that every serving one had to be
in the proper order.

4. David and the Leaders of the Army
Setting Apart Some of the Sons
of Asaph, Heman, and Jeduthun

David and the leaders of the army set apart some of the
sons of Asaph, Heman (a descendant of the great rebel
Korah—Num. 16—and a grandson of Samuel—1 Chron. 6:33),
and Jeduthun, appointed by King David as the leaders, to
prophesy (to sing) with lyres, harps, and cymbals, and divided
them into twenty-four divisions (ch. 25). To sing praises to

God was the main part of Israel's worship to God (cf. Eph. 5:19). Today we need to have more singing of praises to God.

5. The Doorkeepers
Being Divided into Divisions

The doorkeepers, some of whom were the descendants of Korah the great rebel, were divided into divisions to keep the gates of the temple on the east, north, south, and west, and the gate of the storehouse (1 Chron. 26:1-19).

6. Of the Levites, Some Being Assigned
to Keep the Treasures of the House of God

Of the Levites, some were assigned to keep the treasures of the house of God and the treasures of the dedicated gifts dedicated by David the king and the heads and the captains out of the spoil won in battles, for the repair of the house of Jehovah, and all that Samuel, Saul, Abner, and Joab had dedicated (vv. 20-28). This shows that whereas David prepared the materials for the building of the temple, others gained spoil through their victory over the enemies and then offered this spoil to God for the maintenance of the house of God. This can be compared to the situation with the church today. In a sense the church has already been built by Christ through His apostles, and now we are simply maintaining, or repairing, what has been built.

7. Of the Levites, Some Being Appointed
to Outward Duties

Of the Levites, some were appointed to the outward duties over Israel, as officers and judges (vv. 29-32).

8. David's Arrangement
Typifying the Spirit's Arrangement

David's arrangement in order of Israel's services to God related to the temple of God typifies the Spirit's arrangement in order of the church services in the New Testament (1 Cor. 12:4-11; 14:40).

V. THE OFFICERS IN THE ADMINISTRATION OF DAVID'S GOVERNMENT

First Chronicles 27 speaks of the officers in the administration of David's government.

A. The Officers Who Served the King Being of Twelve Divisions

The officers who served the king were of twelve divisions, twenty-four thousand in each division, taking care of the king's affairs month by month throughout all the months of the year (vv. 1-15). This was excessive, and it might have been a hidden factor in the rebellion after the time of Solomon. Any enjoyment that is too luxurious cannot last. Today no one should have an enjoyment that is excessive and too luxurious.

B. Thirteen Captains Ruling over the Twelve Tribes and the House of Aaron

Thirteen captains ruled over the twelve tribes and the house of Aaron (vv. 16-22). Here we should note that David did not take the number of the children of Israel from twenty years old and under because of the fear of the wrath of God (vv. 23-24). David's numbering of the people had offended God (2 Sam. 24), and thus he did not dare to count the younger ones.

C. There Being Officers over the King's Treasures

There were officers over the king's treasures and overseers of the property that belonged to the king (1 Chron. 27:25-31).

D. David Having Counselors, Teachers, Friends, and the Captain of His Army

David had counselors, teachers, friends, and the captain of his army (vv. 32-34).

E. Typifying the Submission to the Authority and Headship of Christ in the Church

The governmental order in David's administration typifies the submission to the authority and headship of Christ in the church in the New Testament (1 Cor. 11:3; Eph. 4:15).

VI. DAVID'S ASSEMBLING AT JERUSALEM
ALL THE LEADERS OF ISRAEL

First Chronicles 28 and 29 are a record of David's assembling at Jerusalem all the leaders of Israel.

A. His Address to the Assembly

In 28:2-8 we have David's address to the assembly.

1. Introducing His Son Solomon
to Be the Builder of the Temple of God

David introduced his son Solomon to be the builder of the temple of God (vv. 2-7). David said that he had it in his heart to build a house for Jehovah. However, Jehovah told him that he would not build a house for His name but that Solomon his son would build His house (vv. 2-3, 6).

2. Charging Them to Observe
All the Commandments of Jehovah

David charged the leaders to observe all the commandments of Jehovah in order that they might possess the good land and leave it as an inheritance forever to their children (v. 8). If they behaved properly before God, they would enjoy the land and leave the land as an inheritance to their children.

B. Charging Solomon His Son
to Serve God and
to Build the Temple of God

In verses 9 through 21 David charged Solomon his son to serve God and to build the temple of God. He charged Solomon to serve God with his "whole heart and with a willing soul, for Jehovah searches all the hearts and understands every imagination of the thoughts" (v. 9). Then David charged Solomon to build the temple of God according to the pattern that he had by the Spirit, having God's presence, with the priests, the Levites, the willing men with wisdom for any service, the leaders, and all the people wholly at his command (vv. 10-21).

C. His Preparation of the Materials and His Gifts for the Building of the Temple of God Stirring Up the Leaders of Israel to Offer Willingly to God

David's preparation of the materials and his gifts for the building of the temple of God stirred up the leaders of Israel to offer willingly their gifts to God for the building of His temple, so that both the people of Israel and David the king rejoiced with great joy (29:1-9). In this matter David and the leaders of Israel were one.

D. His Blessing to Jehovah in the Sight of All the Assembly

Verses 10 through 19 are David's blessing to Jehovah in the sight of all the assembly.

1. Praising God

First, David praised God for His greatness, power, splendor, victory, and majesty (vv. 10-12).

2. Thanking God

Next, David thanked God that it was of Him that he and the people could willingly offer back to God all things which they had received from Him (vv. 13-17). They had received so much from God, and what they had received they offered back to God for the building of the house of God.

3. Asking God

David continued by asking God to keep and establish the heart of His people Israel in this sound condition and give Solomon his son a wholeness of heart to keep God's commandments, testimonies, and statutes and to do all and build the palace (the temple) of God (vv. 18-19).

E. The Response of All the Assembly

Verses 20 through 25 describe the response of all the assembly.

1. Blessing Jehovah

The people blessed Jehovah, offered sacrifices to Him, and worshipped Him (vv. 20-21).

2. Eating and Drinking before Jehovah and Making Solomon the Son of David King a Second Time

The people ate and drank before Jehovah and made Solomon the son of David king a second time. All Israel obeyed him, with all the leaders and mighty men and all the sons of King David submitting themselves to Solomon the king. Jehovah magnified Solomon exceedingly in the sight of all Israel and bestowed upon him a royal majesty that had never been on any king before him over Israel (vv. 22-25).

F. David Dying at a Good Old Age

David died at a good old age, full of days, riches, and honor (v. 28).

Although we need to know these historical matters, I do not have much burden concerning them, for they are not the center, the reality, the goal, of the Bible. The center, the reality, and the goal of the Bible is God's economy. God's economy is that God would become a man to make man God in life and in nature but not in the Godhead for the producing of the New Jerusalem as the increase and expression of the Triune God for eternity. The New Jerusalem is built by God's constituting Himself into man to make man the same as God in life, in nature, and in constitution so that God and man may become a corporate entity.

LIFE-STUDY OF FIRST AND SECOND CHRONICLES

MESSAGE SIX

THE SUPPLEMENT TO THE HISTORY OF THE KINGS OF JUDAH

(1)

Scripture Reading: 2 Chron. 11:5-23; 13:1-21; 14:6—15:15; 17:1-19; 19:1—20:30

The books of 1 and 2 Chronicles are supplements to the other books of history in the Old Testament. In 1 Chronicles there is, first, a supplement to the history of mankind, for 1 and 2 Samuel and 1 and 2 Kings do not include the genealogy of mankind, which is found in 1 Chronicles 1—9. In the previous message we covered the supplement to the history of David. In this message we will begin to consider the supplement to the history of the kings of Judah.

I. OF REHOBOAM

In 2 Chronicles 11:5-23 we have a word concerning the reign of Rehoboam.

A. Being Capable and Wise

Rehoboam was capable and wise (v. 23).

B. Not Laboring for God's Interest on the Earth

Although Rehoboam was capable and wise, he did not labor for God's interest on the earth to build up the kingdom of God. Instead, he worked for his own interest, transmuting the kingdom of God into a monarchy not only for himself but also for his descendants (vv. 22-23). For this he lost the greater part of his kingdom. The kingdom of his father Solomon was glorious and splendid, but not long after Rehoboam began to reign, he lost nearly the entire kingdom. This loss was due to his failure to labor for God's interest.

C. His Way and Condition Not Being Proper

Rehoboam's kingdom was on the proper ground of oneness according to God's choice of a unique place (Deut. 12:13-14), and he was fundamental and not apostate, but the way he took and the condition he worked out were not proper. He remained on the proper ground in Jerusalem and he believed and kept the teachings of Moses according to God's revelation. He did not leave God's truth and God's speaking, but he labored for his own interest, not for God's interest.

All the elders should pay attention to this. Elders, you are on the proper ground and you may be fundamental, but for what are you laboring? Are you laboring for God's interest or for your own interest? If you are for your interest, you make the local church a monarchy, your own little empire, not a part of the kingdom of God.

D. The Priests and the Levites throughout All Israel Abandoning Their Property and Going to Judah and Jerusalem

Due to the proper ground of Rehoboam's kingdom and his fundamental faith, the priests and the Levites throughout all Israel abandoned their property and went to Judah and Jerusalem. Those from all the tribes of Israel who set their hearts to seek Jehovah came with the Levites to Jerusalem to sacrifice (that is, to offer their offerings) to the God of their fathers, thus strengthening the kingdom of Judah and supporting Rehoboam the son of Solomon for three years, for they walked in the way of David and Solomon for three years (vv. 13-17). Taking the proper ground and keeping the fundamental faith attracted the seekers of God, and they went to Jerusalem to join Rehoboam for the kingdom of God. However, actually he was not for the kingdom of God; he was for his own monarchy.

E. Rehoboam Indulging His Sexual Lust

Rehoboam indulged his sexual lust by taking eighteen

wives and sixty concubines and begetting twenty-eight sons and sixty daughters, and he sought for his sons many wives (vv. 21, 23). This brought in corruption to them, to their descendants, and to their monarchy. Although Rehoboam took the proper ground and was fundamental, he lived a life of the indulgence of lust. In this matter he was surely influenced by his father, who had hundreds of wives and concubines.

II. OF ABIJAH

Second Chronicles 13:1-21 gives us an account of the reign of Abijah.

A. Defeating Jeroboam the King of Israel

Abijah defeated Jeroboam the king of Israel (vv. 2b-20). In this matter Abijah was quite good.

1. Proclaiming the Apostasy of Jeroboam

Abijah proclaimed to Jeroboam and all Israel the apostasy of Jeroboam. Abijah and Judah took the fundamental standing, and Abijah advised Jeroboam not to fight against them with whom Jehovah stood (vv. 4-12). Here we see that Abijah stood on the fundamental ground to make a proclamation.

2. Jeroboam and the Children of Israel Being Defeated

Jeroboam and the children of Israel were defeated by Abijah and the children of Judah, and Jehovah struck Jeroboam to death (vv. 13-20). This indicates that Jehovah stood with Abijah.

B. Indulging in Sexual Lust

Abijah also indulged in sexual lust by marrying fourteen wives and begetting twenty-two sons and sixteen daughters (v. 21).

III. OF ASA

In 14:6—15:15 we have an account of the reign of Asa.

A. Asa Building Fortress Cities in Judah

Asa built fortress cities in Judah, for the land was quiet and there was no war against him during those years, because Jehovah had given him rest (14:6-8). Asa was good, and God was pleased with him.

B. Asa Defeating the Cushites

Asa defeated the Cushites by calling out to God and trusting in Him (vv. 9-15).

C. Asa's Further Reforms

Asa carried out some further reforms (15:1-15). These reforms were in addition to those mentioned in 14:3-5 and 15:16, 18.

1. Through the Advice and Encouragement of the Prophet Azariah

Asa's further reforms were accomplished through the advice and encouragement of the prophet Azariah the son of Oded (15:1-7).

2. Putting Away the Abominations from All the Land of Judah and Benjamin

Asa put away the abominations (the idols) from all the land of Judah and Benjamin and from the cities that he had taken in the hill country of Ephraim and restored the altar of Jehovah (v. 8). The people had fallen to such an extent that they had given up the altar of God and had built altars for the worship of idols. But Asa dealt with that situation.

3. Gathering All Judah and Benjamin and All the Sojourners with Them from Ephraim, Manasseh, and Simeon

Asa gathered all Judah and Benjamin and all the sojourners with them from Ephraim, Manasseh, and Simeon (for many from Israel threw in their lot with him when they saw that Jehovah his God was with him), and they sacrificed to Jehovah from the spoil. They also entered into a covenant to pursue Jehovah and covenanted that anyone who did not pursue Jehovah would be put to death. Thus Jehovah gave them rest all around (vv. 9-15).

Although Asa was a good king, in chapter sixteen he did some things that were wrong. When Baasha king of Israel went up against Judah, Asa formed an alliance with Ben-hadad king of Syria (16:1-6). Hanani the seer came to Asa and rebuked him for trusting in the king of Syria and not trusting in Jehovah (vv. 7-9). Asa became angry with the seer and put him in prison. At that time Asa also oppressed some of the people (v. 10). In the thirty-ninth year of his reign, Asa became severely diseased in his feet, "yet even in his disease he pursued not Jehovah but the physicians" (v. 12). Eventually, Asa died in the forty-first year of his reign (vv. 13-14).

IV. OF JEHOSHAPHAT

Second Chronicles 17:1-19 and 19:1—20:30 are concerned with the reign of Jehoshaphat.

A. Strengthening Himself against Israel

Jehoshaphat strengthened himself against Israel and put forces in all the fortified cities of Judah and put garrisons in the land of Judah and in the cities of Ephraim that Asa his father had taken (17:1-2).

B. Jehovah Being with Him Because He Walked in the Ways of David His Father

Jehovah was with Jehoshaphat because he walked in the former ways of David and did not pursue the Baals, the idols, and removed the high places and the Asherim from Judah. All Judah gave tribute to him, and he had riches and honor in abundance (vv. 3-6). In this record we see a principle that God keeps. This principle is that to whoever behaves before Him God gives rest to enjoy the good land.

C. Establishing the Kingdom of God

Jehoshaphat established the kingdom of God by sending

his officials, the Levites, and the priests to teach the children of Judah by the book of the law of Jehovah (vv. 7-9).

D. Jehovah Causing All the Kingdoms around Judah to Fear Jehoshaphat and Give Him Tribute

Jehovah caused all the kingdoms around Judah to fear Jehoshaphat and give him tribute, so that he grew exceedingly great and built a strong national defense and a great army of 1,160,000 mighty men of valor (vv. 10-19). That means that he was strong and that in his kingship he enjoyed the good land.

E. Rebuked by Jehu the Seer for Helping Ahab

Jehoshaphat was rebuked by Jehu the seer for helping Ahab, the evil king of Israel (19:1-3; cf. ch. 18).

F. Setting Up Judges throughout All the Fortified Cities of Judah to Take Care of All the Cases of the People

Jehoshaphat set up judges throughout all the fortified cities of Judah to take care of the cases of the people. The judges were under Amariah the chief priest in all matters concerning Jehovah and under Zebadiah the ruler of the house of Judah in all matters concerning the king, with the Levites serving them as officers (19:4-11). Here we see a healthy situation. There was a good priest taking care of the worship of God and a good ruler taking care of governmental matters. In addition, the Levites were faithful to Jehoshaphat. In such a healthy situation, Jehoshaphat enjoyed the good land because he feared God.

G. Defeating the Army of the Children of Ammon, Moab, and Mount Seir by Trusting in Jehovah

In 20:1-30 we see that Jehoshaphat defeated the great army of the children of Ammon, Moab, and Mount Seir by trusting in Jehovah.

1. Setting His Face to Pursue Jehovah

Jehoshaphat set his face to pursue Jehovah and proclaimed a fast throughout all Judah, and all the cities of
Judah came to seek Jehovah (vv. 3-4). It was very good that he
proclaimed a fast that the people would have a time to pray
about their situation.

2. Praying to Jehovah in the Assembly

Jehoshaphat prayed to Jehovah in the assembly of Judah
and Jerusalem with their little ones, wives, and children
(vv. 5-13).

3. Jehovah Answering His Prayer
through Jahaziel, a Levite

Jehovah answered Jehoshaphat's prayer through Jahaziel,
a Levite. Jehoshaphat and all Judah and the inhabitants of
Jerusalem worshipped Jehovah, with the Levites praising
Jehovah, the God of Israel, with an exceedingly loud voice
(vv. 14-19).

4. Jehovah Destroying
and Demolishing Their Enemy

The next morning they went to meet the enemy with
the encouragement of their king Jehoshaphat: "Believe in
Jehovah your God, and you will be established; believe in His
prophets, and you will succeed" (v. 20). They went also with
the singers giving thanks in holy array before the army.
Then Jehovah destroyed and demolished their enemy; and
Jehoshaphat and his people gathered the spoil in abundance,
more than they could carry, for three days. They came back to
Jerusalem with harps, lyres, and trumpets to enter the house
of Jehovah. This surely was a triumphant celebration. Thus
the kingdom of Jehoshaphat was quiet, for his God had given
him rest all around (vv. 21-30).

From the cases of the kings covered in this message, we
need to learn to be very careful to behave ourselves properly.
God is great, but He also cares about all the details. We may
be right in big things, but we may be wrong in small things, in

the details. We should not think that it is a small thing to be wrong in the small things. In principle, to be wrong in anything, great or small, is a serious matter. In the record of God's dealing with these kings of Judah, God took every detail of their behavior, even if it was quite small, as a reason to discipline them.

LIFE-STUDY OF FIRST
AND SECOND CHRONICLES

BEING FUNDAMENTAL IN FULL AND WALKING
ACCORDING TO THE ALL-INCLUSIVE SPIRIT

Scripture Reading: 2 Chron. 11:5, 13-14; Rom. 8:4; Gal. 5:16,
25

In this message I would like to say a word about our need
to be fundamental in a full and complete way and also about
our need in our daily living to walk according to the compound, all-inclusive, life-giving Spirit.

STANDING ON THE PROPER GROUND
AND KEEPING THE FUNDAMENTAL FAITH

I thank God that in 1 and 2 Chronicles there is a record
showing us how God deals with His people in detail. God's
dealing with His people in the details of their living is for His
people to enjoy the good land, Christ, in a very proper way. To
enjoy the good land, the kings had to stand on the proper
ground and they had to be fundamental, keeping the faith
given by God through Moses.

It is the same with us today. The church ground is quite
important, and to keep all the truths, to be fundamental, is
also important. Today's Christians claim to be fundamental,
but they are fundamental only in part. They are not fundamental in full. Through the years we have been trying our
best, by God's mercy and grace, to be perfectly fundamental,
that is, to be fundamental not just in part but in full.

THE TRUTH CONCERNING THE ASSURANCE
OF SALVATION AND THE TRUTH
CONCERNING CHRIST AS LIFE

Brother Watchman Nee, who was raised up by the Lord
more than seventy years ago, read the Bible thoroughly again

and again. The hundreds of missionaries who came to China from Europe and America were faithful in a sense, but they did not make clear to the Chinese Christians the basic truth of the assurance of salvation. The missionaries translated the Bible, preached from the Bible, and taught the Bible, but they did not point out that the believers in Christ could have and should have the assurance of their salvation. After Brother Nee was raised up by the Lord, he preached and taught the truth concerning the assurance of salvation, and I followed him to do this. Wherever we went we asked people if they knew whether or not they were saved. When we would ask this question, the pastors and preachers would laugh at us and tell us that we were proud for saying that we knew that we were saved. In this situation Brother Nee fought the battle for the truth concerning the assurance of salvation. Today millions of Chinese Christians everywhere believe in the assurance of salvation. They know that as long as they believe in the Lord Jesus, they are saved and may have the assurance that they have been saved. The situation now is very different from the situation when Brother Nee began to fight for this basic truth.

Brother Nee continued to fight for the truth, and eventually he released the truth regarding Christ as our life and our taking Christ as life. This was another truth which the missionaries in China did not make clear to the believers. Once the believers have the assurance of their salvation, they need to see that they have Christ in them as their life and that they should take Christ as their life and live by Christ.

THE TRUTH CONCERNING THE NEW JERUSALEM

During the past seventy-two years, in His recovery the Lord has gone on and on to recover many other truths. In particular, the Lord has recovered the truth concerning the New Jerusalem in Revelation 21 and 22. Many expositors of the Bible do not have the proper understanding of what the New Jerusalem is. Very few Bible teachers have written anything about the spiritual significance of the New Jerusalem. Among these few are a German teacher from long ago named Tersteegen and our dear friend T. Austin-Sparks, whom I regard as the last of the inner-life teachers. Like Tersteegen, T. Austin-Sparks saw that the New Jerusalem is not a physical city but a sign with a spiritual significance. Brother Sparks pointed out that the spiritual things concerning God, Christ, and the church are mysterious and that God uses signs to reveal the truth regarding such spiritual things. We took his word and still hold to it.

The book of Revelation opens with a word about signs: "The revelation of Jesus Christ which God gave to Him to show to His slaves the things that must quickly take place; and He made it known by signs, sending it by His angel to His slave John." This indicates that the revelation in this book is composed of signs, that is, symbols with a spiritual significance, such as the seven lampstands, signifying the seven churches, and the Lamb, signifying Christ the Redeemer as the unique sacrifice to accomplish God's eternal redemption. Even the New Jerusalem is a sign, the last and consummate sign, signifying the ultimate consummation of God's economy. In the last fifty years, the truth concerning the New Jerusalem has become more and more clear to us. As a result, in our hymnal there are a number of hymns on the New Jerusalem.

THE TRUTH CONCERNING DEIFICATION—THAT GOD BECAME A MAN THAT MAN MAY BECOME GOD IN LIFE AND IN NATURE BUT NOT IN THE GODHEAD

If we would be fundamental in full, we must be fundamental with respect to all the truths. Among the many truths there are three great mysteries which were discovered by the church fathers in the second century: the mystery of the Divine Trinity, the mystery of Christ's person, and the mystery of man's deification—that God became a man that man may become God in life and in nature but not in the Godhead. Although Christians hold the truth concerning the Triune God and the truth concerning the person of Christ, after the first five centuries the truth concerning deification was gradually lost. In February of this year, I became burdened to release messages on this truth.

After I began to speak concerning God becoming a man that man may become God in life and in nature, I learned that the Catholic Church is also paying attention to this matter of deification. Not long ago a brother showed me that the *Catechism of the Catholic Church,* recently published by the Roman Catholic Church, presents the following:

ARTICLE 3

"HE WAS CONCEIVED BY THE POWER OF THE HOLY SPIRIT, AND WAS BORN OF THE VIRGIN MARY"

Paragraph 1. The Son of God Became Man

I.   WHY DID THE WORD BECOME FLESH?

460   The Word became flesh to make us *"partakers of the divine nature"* (2 Pet. 1:4): "For this is why the Word became man, and the Son of God became the Son of man: so that man, by entering into communion with the Word and thus receiving divine sonship, might become a son of God" (St. Irenaeus, *Adv. haeres.* 3, 19, 1). "For the Son of God became man so that we might become God" (St. Athanasius, *De inc.,* 54, 3). *"The only-begotten Son of God, wanting to make us sharers in his divinity, assumed our nature, so that he, made man, might make men gods"* (St. Thomas Aquinas, *Opusc.* 57:1-4). (*Catechism of the Catholic Church,* pp. 115-116).

Here we see that the Catholic Church teaches that the believers in Christ can become God. Furthermore, another brother told me about a book, written in Arabic by a Catholic priest, which says the same thing about man becoming God. In order to be perfectly fundamental, we need to be clear concerning this great truth—the truth that God became a man that man may become God in life and in nature but not in the Godhead.

CONDUCTING OURSELVES ACCORDING TO THE SPIRIT

However, it is not adequate just to have the proper ground and to be perfectly fundamental. What we are, how we live, and how we behave mean a lot. God's people in the Old Testament received of God through Moses a set of books called the law. Today God is dealing with us not according to the law but according to the compound, life-giving, indwelling, consummated Spirit. In the Old Testament time, God's people were required to behave themselves according to the law. Today we are required by the New Testament to conduct ourselves according to the compound, life-giving, all-inclusive Spirit (Rom. 8:4).

God dealt with all the good kings of Judah according to the law of Moses in detail. Anyone who was wrong with the law even a little would lose a great part of the enjoyment of the good land. This typifies and signifies that today we must conduct ourselves according to the spiritual law, and the spiritual law is just the Spirit Himself, the compound Spirit.

We need to be careful in every detail. For instance, when we talk to our spouse, we have to talk according to the spirit. We need to walk in all things according to the spirit (Rom. 8:4). We need to be warned and be on the alert that whatever we say, whatever we do, whatever we express, our attitude, our spirit, and our intention must be purified by the life-giving, compound, all-inclusive Spirit. Otherwise, we will lose much in the enjoyment of Christ, today's good land.

Now we are studying the books of history in the Old Testament. We need to learn the lessons from all the details recorded in these books. Consider the case of Asa. He was a good king and he did many good things. However, he offended God by forming an alliance with Ben-hadad king of Syria (2 Chron. 16:1-6). Furthermore, he became angry with the seer who rebuked him for trusting in the king of Syria instead of trusting in Jehovah. It might have been because of this offense that Asa became severely diseased in his feet. This disease caused his death (vv. 7-10, 12-13).

From the cases recorded in the books of history, we see that God is not only loving but also fearful. Therefore, as Paul says in Philippians 2:12, we must learn to work out our own salvation with fear and trembling.

LIFE-STUDY OF FIRST
AND SECOND CHRONICLES

MESSAGE EIGHT

LEARNING FROM THE EXAMPLES
OF THE KINGS OF JUDAH
TO HAVE A GOD-MAN LIVING IN OUR DAILY LIFE

Scripture Reading: 2 Chron. 3:1; 11:5, 13-16; 15:9-10; 2 Cor.
3:17-18; Rom. 8:29; Phil. 3:13-14; Rom. 5:17b, 21b

Prayer: Lord, how we thank You for a time to be with You
and with saints from around the globe. What a chance, Lord,
to have a blending not only among ourselves but also a blending with You. Hallelujah, what a blending that we, the
tripartite man, can be blended with the Triune God! Lord,
give us a heart to treasure this time. We would not let You go
and we would not let ourselves go until we have some blending with You. We believe that we are under Your anointing,
the anointing of the compound, all-inclusive, life-giving
Spirit, who is the consummation of the Triune God dwelling
within us. Lord, we praise You that we are living in this most
blessed day, the day that will close this age and bring You
back. Lord, thank You for Your presence. Thank You for open-
ing up Your Word. Thank You that we have not only the
printed Word but also the opened and interpreted Word. Your
Word has been opened up to us, and You are waiting for us to
take it. Help us, Lord. We are weak, we are nothing, and we
need You. Amen.

THE KINGS OF JUDAH
STANDING ON THE PROPER GROUND

The supplement to the history of the kings of Judah
recorded in 2 Chronicles shows us that the kings in Judah
stood on the proper ground—Jerusalem—the ground chosen,
ordained, and established by God (Deut. 12:5-18). God's

choosing of this ground according to His ordination is clearly seen in Deuteronomy 12, a chapter that we need to study carefully.

Jerusalem is the place chosen by God to be His worship center for the whole earth. Today statesmen and world leaders are debating about who the rightful owner of Jerusalem is. This debate is foolish, and those who are debating do not know what they are talking about, for they do not know that God is the owner of Jerusalem. Jerusalem, the center of God's worship, belongs to the Triune God.

We may say that God's choice of Jerusalem as the worship center began with His word to Abraham in Genesis 22:2. God told Abraham to go to the land of Moriah and to offer Isaac (a type of Christ) upon one of the mountains of which God would tell him. The place—Mount Moriah—where Abraham offered Isaac was also the site—Mount Zion—selected by God for the temple (2 Chron. 3:1; 2 Sam. 24:25). Zion is actually a peak of Mount Moriah. When Solomon was about to build the temple, there was no need for him to select a place because the place had already been selected by God and made known to David. I believe that this site was the very spot where Isaac was offered to God by his father. The choice of this place was God's ordination.

The kings of Judah remained on the proper ground, Jerusalem, chosen by God, but the kings of Israel abandoned the God-ordained ground. Jeroboam even set up other worship centers in Bethel and Dan (1 Kings 12:29-30). This action was an abomination in the eyes of the Lord. The kings of Judah were right with respect to the ground. The proper ground, the unique ground, the ground chosen, ordained, and established by God, signifies the ground on which we should practice the church life today.

THE KINGS OF JUDAH KEEPING
THEIR FUNDAMENTAL FAITH IN GOD'S WORD

The kings of Judah also kept their belief in the Word of God given by Moses. Therefore, regarding their faith they were fundamental. Thus the kings of Judah were right in two things: remaining on the proper ground and keeping the fundamental faith in God's Word.

ATTRACTING TO JERUSALEM THE PRIESTS, THE LEVITES, AND THOSE FROM ALL THE TRIBES WHO SET THEIR HEARTS TO SEEK JEHOVAH

The proper ground and the fundamental faith were attractions for a good number of God's people, especially the priests and the Levites. During the reign of Rehoboam, the Levites abandoned their pasture lands and their property and went to Jerusalem (2 Chron. 11:13-14). Moreover, "those from all the tribes of Israel who set their hearts to seek Jehovah, the God of Israel, came after them to Jerusalem to sacrifice to Jehovah, the God of their fathers" (v. 16). Not only the priests and Levites but all those who sought Jehovah in other tribes gave up their property and came to the worship center in Jerusalem. Later, during the reign of Asa, "many from Israel threw in their lot with him when they saw that Jehovah his God was with him" (15:9). They were attracted to Jerusalem because the kings of Judah stood on the proper ground and kept the fundamental faith.

However, this is not all that we should have. We have seen that the kings of Judah were on the proper ground of Jerusalem and that they kept the fundamental faith, but now we need to consider how they behaved themselves.

EXAMPLES REFERRING TO THE WAY WE CONDUCT OURSELVES IN THE DETAILS OF OUR DAILY LIVING

In the Old Testament history books we can see many different pictures, but we may not have an accurate interpretation of these pictures. The correct interpretation of the pictures in the history of the kings of Judah recorded in the books of Chronicles is that these kings are examples showing us that it is not sufficient for us who love God and seek Christ only to stand on the right ground and keep the fundamental truth. We also need to take care of who we are, how we behave, and how we conduct ourselves. We must also pay attention to our interest, our intention, our purpose, our goal, our attitude, and our way of speaking. For example, we should pay attention to the tone of our voice. Sometimes our tone of voice may be like that of a roaring lion, not like that of a God-man.

The books of 1 and 2 Chronicles give us many examples of how the kings of Judah conducted themselves in the good land. These examples show how they were, how they behaved themselves, how they did things, how they faced different situations, what their intentions were, what their interests were, and what their goals were as kings in the good land. These examples refer to the way we conduct ourselves in the details of our daily living.

Consider the daily situation in your married life. You are on the proper ground of the church and you keep the fundamental faith, but how do you speak to your spouse? How do you treat your spouse? What is your attitude toward your wife or husband? In your married life do you walk according to the spirit or according to something else? Do you live the life of a God-man with your husband or wife?

In order to live the life of a God-man, we must be crucified. We must be dying to live. If we live a crucified life in our married life, then in our married life we will have the living of a God-man.

Many saints are very good in the church meetings and in the church service, but at home they may live the life not of a God-man but of a "scorpion-man," exchanging words or quarreling. A certain couple may love the Lord and His recovery. However, at dinner the husband may criticize his wife for her attitude, and she may condemn him for his way of speaking. Then after dinner they attend the meeting of their vital group. But how can these two "scorpions" be vital? Because of such a daily situation, in this country it is very difficult to find a genuine vital group. According to my observation, in the vital groups I have seen only deadness, not vitality. All the vital members should be God-men, crucified in their natural life to live a God-man life by the divine life within them.

WHAT THE LORD WANTS TODAY

My burden in these messages is not to teach biblical

history. Rather, my burden is to minister what the Lord wants today. The Lord desires that many of His believers would gradually be transformed into God-men. Second Corinthians 3:17 says that the Lord is the Spirit. Verse 18 goes on to say, "We all with unveiled face, beholding and reflecting like a mirror the glory of the Lord, are being transformed into the same image from glory to glory, even as from the Lord Spirit." This means that we should keep our face unveiled and look at the Lord that we may be transformed into His image. Transformation requires a process; it cannot take place overnight. Furthermore, Romans 8:29 says God has predestinated us not just to be transformed but also to be conformed to the image of His Son, that this Son might be the Firstborn among many brothers. My burden is that we, the believers in Christ, would gradually be transformed and conformed to be God-men.

THE ENJOYMENT OF CHRIST DIFFERING IN DEGREES

In the first message we pointed out that our enjoyment of Christ differs in degrees according to our pursuing of Christ and our faithfulness to Him. The highest attainment of pursuing Christ is to reign with Christ in His divine life through His abounding grace (Phil. 3:13-14; Rom. 5:17b, 21b). Our pursuing of Christ and our faithfulness to Him determine how much we enjoy Him. To have the highest attainment in pursuing Christ is to reign with Him as kings in His divine life.

The kings of Judah attained to a position where they could enjoy the good land of Canaan in their kingship. They were kings to enjoy the good land. The extent of their enjoyment depended on what they were, on how they behaved themselves, and on what their goals, interests, and intentions were. We need to learn from their examples how to have a God-man living in all the details of our daily life.

LIFE-STUDY OF FIRST AND SECOND CHRONICLES

MESSAGE NINE

THE SUPPLEMENT TO THE HISTORY OF THE KINGS OF JUDAH

(2)

Scripture Reading: 2 Chron. 21:12-18; 24:14b-24; 25:5-16; 26:6-21a; 28:8-15

In our study of the supplement to the history of the kings of Judah, we are covering only twelve of the twenty kings of Judah because only the supplementary matters related to these twelve were not covered in 1 and 2 Kings. Furthermore, in this supplement in 1 and 2 Chronicles none of the kings of Israel are included, because they all forsook both the proper ground, the ground of Jerusalem, and the fundamental faith given by God through Moses. Thus, God forsook them because of their apostasy.

In this message we will continue to consider the supplement to the history of the kings of Judah, looking at the examples of Jehoram, Joash, Amaziah, Uzziah, and Ahaz.

V. OF JEHORAM

In 2 Chronicles 21:12-18 we have a word concerning Jehoram.

A. Warned by Elijah the Prophet

Jehoram, a descendant of David and Solomon, was warned by Elijah the prophet concerning his evils before God and his miserable end (vv. 12-15). Jehoram stood on the proper ground and he kept the fundamental faith, but he was evil in the sight of God. Because of this, Elijah told him that his life would come to a miserable end.

B. Jehovah Stirring Up
the Philistines and Arabians against Him

Jehovah stirred up the Philistines and Arabians against
Jehoram. They came up against Judah, broke through into it,
and carried away all the possessions of his house as well as
his sons and his wives, except Jehoahaz, the youngest of his
sons (vv. 16-17). What a miserable end to Jehoram's enjoyment of the good land in his kingship. His reign should have
been glorious and splendid, but instead it was miserable.
Everything and everyone was captured, including his wives
and his sons. But in His mercy the Lord spared the youngest
son to continue the throne.

C. Jehovah Striking Him with an Incurable Illness

After all this, Jehovah struck Jehoram in his bowels with
an incurable illness (v. 18). This illness might have been
cancer.

VI. OF JOASH

In 24:14b-24 we have an account of the reign of Joash.

A. Seeing the Good Pattern of the Chief Priest

Joash saw the good pattern of the chief priest Jehoiada
of doing well in Israel and with God and restoring the house
of God; and Jehoiada had shown him kindness in raising
him up to be the prince to succeed the throne of David
(vv. 14b-16, 22a). This means this high priest protected the
royal family. He did well in three directions: with the people,
with God, and with the house of God, keeping the house of
God during a time of rebellion.

B. Listening to the Captains of Judah
and Forsaking the House of Jehovah

After the death of the chief priest Jehoiada, Joash listened
to the captains of Judah, the leaders of the army, and forsook
the house of Jehovah the God of their fathers and served the
Asherim and the idols, bringing in the wrath of God upon
Judah and Jerusalem (vv. 17-18).

C. God Sending Prophets
to the People of Judah and Jerusalem
to Bring Them Back to Jehovah

In His mercy, God still sent prophets to the people of Judah and Jerusalem to bring them back to Jehovah. The Spirit of God clothed (that is, was poured upon) Zechariah the son of Jehoiada the chief priest to testify to them that they did not prosper because they transgressed the commandments of Jehovah. Joash the king, not remembering the kindness which Jehoiada the father of Zechariah had shown him, commanded the conspiring people to stone him to death in the court of the house of Jehovah (vv. 19-22).

D. The Army of the Syrians
Coming Up against Him

At the turn of the year, the army of the Syrians came up against Joash and came to Judah and Jerusalem and destroyed all the leaders of the people. This took place even though the number of the Syrian army was smaller than that of the very great army of Judah (vv. 23-24a). This defeat of a great army by a smaller army was of God. It was God's discipline of His people that they would learn how to enjoy the riches of the good land in full and live a long life there in peace.

In God's mercy, Joash was the only one of his father's sons to be spared. He was then raised up by the great priest Jehoiada to be the prince. At the beginning of his reign he was good, and he remembered what Jehoiada had done for him. But when Jehoiada died, he listened to the leaders of the military power which came in. He was subdued by them and he followed them to worship the idols, and so forth. Eventually he conspired to martyr Zechariah, the son of the very one who had taken such good care of him. Forgetting all the kindness that had been shown to him, Joash was in company with those who conspired to put the son of Jehoiada to death. The next year the Syrian army came "because they had forsaken Jehovah the God of their fathers. Thus they executed judgment on Joash" (v. 24b).

VII. OF AMAZIAH

In 25:5-16 we have the example of Amaziah.

A. Preparing Three Hundred Thousand Chosen Men for War

Amaziah prepared three hundred thousand chosen men for war and hired from Israel one hundred thousand mighty men of valor to fight against the Edomites (vv. 5-6).

B. A Man of God Advising Amaziah Not to Fight with the Help of the Army of Israel

A man of God advised Amaziah not to fight with the help of the army of Israel, because God was not with Israel. Then he let the army of Israel go back to their own place, and their anger was greatly kindled against Judah (vv. 7-10).

C. Strengthening Himself to Fight the Children of Edom

Amaziah strengthened himself to fight the children of Edom with his own people and defeated them, capturing some of them (vv. 11-12). Here Amaziah had a clear standing and therefore was able to fight against Edom.

D. The Men of Israel Whom Amaziah Sent Back Raiding the Cities of Judah

The men of Israel whom Amaziah had sent back from going with him into battle raided the cities of Judah, killed three thousand of them, and took much spoil (v. 13).

E. Setting Up the Gods of the Edomites as His Gods for Worship

After Amaziah defeated the Edomites, he brought their gods and set them up as his gods for worship. This was his great failure. The anger of Jehovah was kindled against him, and He sent a prophet to warn him. But he would not listen to the prophet, and God determined to destroy him (vv. 14-16).

VIII. OF UZZIAH (AZARIAH)

Second Chronicles 26:6-21a speaks of the reign of Uzziah, whose other name is Azariah.

A. Defeating the Philistines, the Arabians, and the Meunim by the Help of God

Uzziah defeated the Philistines, the Arabians, and the Meunim by the help of God, and the Ammonites gave tribute to him. His fame went as far as Egypt. Thus he became exceedingly strong (vv. 6-8). This shows us that if we go along with the very God whom we worship, we will prosper. Otherwise, we will suffer.

B. Building Towers in Jerusalem and Works of Defense

Uzziah built towers in Jerusalem and works of defense and hewed out many cisterns for his ranch and farm. He had a mighty army and became strong by the marvelous help of God (vv. 9-15).

C. His Heart Becoming Uplifted to Trespass against Jehovah and Go into the Temple of Jehovah to Burn Incense

When Uzziah became strong, his heart became uplifted to trespass against Jehovah and go into the temple of Jehovah to burn incense (v. 16). You may think that it was not wrong for the king to burn incense. But according to God's ordination in the Old Testament, the kings were not allowed to touch the duties of the priests. Burning the incense was the duty of the priests, not of the kings. Uzziah, however, was proud and did not care for anyone other than himself. Therefore, he went into the temple to do the service of a priest. Azariah the priest, with eighty priests of valor, withstood him to stop him from burning incense to God. Uzziah became angry with the priests, and leprosy broke out on his forehead before the priests. Because of the uncleanness of his leprosy, the priests rushed him out of the temple of God and put him in a separate house as a leper until the day of his death (vv. 17-21a). Here in the case of Uzziah we have another example of a king who had a miserable end.

IX. OF AHAZ

In 28:8-15 we have an account of the reign of Ahaz.

A. Jehovah Delivering Him into the Hand of the King of Israel

When Jehovah delivered Ahaz into the hand of the king of Israel, the children of Israel carried away captive of their brothers two hundred thousand women, sons, and daughters, and also plundered much spoil from them (vv. 5b, 8).

B. Oded, a Prophet of Jehovah, Advising the Children of Israel to Return Their Captives from Judah

Oded, a prophet of Jehovah, came to advise the children of Israel to return their captives from Judah, their brothers, for the burning anger of Jehovah was upon them (vv. 9-11). Oded seemed to be saying that after defeating Ahaz, they should not have captured so many women and young people. God is a God of love, and He would not approve of such a thing. Therefore, His anger was burning upon the people of Israel.

C. The Heads of the Children of Ephraim Returning the Captives to Judah

The heads of the children of Ephraim returned the captives to Judah in a kind and loving way so that they avoided the burning anger of Jehovah upon them (vv. 12-15).

The record in the books of Chronicles reveals that God is just in dealing with His people. Do not think that God will not take the time to deal with you if you are wrong in small things. God has much more time than you have. If you have time to make a mistake, He surely has time to discipline you.

LIFE-STUDY OF FIRST
AND SECOND CHRONICLES

MESSAGE TEN

THE SUPPLEMENT TO THE HISTORY
OF THE KINGS OF JUDAH

(3)

Scripture Reading: 2 Chron. 29:3—32:8; 33:11-17; 34:3-7; 36:20b-23

In previous messages we covered nine kings of Judah who are examples regarding the enjoyment of God's good land, which is a type of the all-inclusive Christ. In this message we will consider three more kings.

X. OF HEZEKIAH

In 29:3—32:8 we have an account of the reign of Hezekiah. He was one of the best kings. But even with Hezekiah there was a hidden defect. This defect is not mentioned in 2 Chronicles, but it is exposed in 2 Kings and in Isaiah.

A. Restoring the House of Jehovah

Hezekiah restored the house of Jehovah and brought out the impurity (things related to idol worship) from the holy place (29:3-36). This was a great thing. The house of God, the temple of God, was the place for His elect to worship Him. But before Hezekiah came into his reign, Israelites put idols into that temple, and in verse 5 these idols are called "the impurity."

1. Charging the Levites and the Priests
to Sanctify the House of Jehovah

Hezekiah charged the Levites and the priests to sanctify the house of Jehovah (vv. 4-11). His charge indicates that after the devastation of the temple, the priests and the Levites were left with nothing to do. Hezekiah charged them to remove from the eyes of the holy God all the idols, all the things of impurity. In verse 11 he said to them, "My sons, do not now be negligent, for Jehovah has chosen you to stand before Him to minister to Him and to be His ministers and burn incense."

2. The Levites and the Priests Doing It according to Hezekiah's Charge

The Levites and the priests did the work of cleansing the temple according to Hezekiah's charge (vv. 12-19).

3. Hezekiah and the Leaders of the City Worshipping God in the House of Jehovah

Hezekiah and the leaders of the city worshipped God in the house of Jehovah (vv. 20-30). This indicates that the temple of God had been left to the idols and that in it there was not the worship of God. Hezekiah took the lead along with the leaders of the city to worship God in the house of Jehovah. In addition, they offered the burnt offering and the sin offering to God with the praising of God by the instruments made by David and with the words of David and Asaph. The burnt offering was for God's satisfaction, and the sin offering was for the forgiveness of their sins.

4. Charging the Assembly of the People to Offer Sacrifices and Thank Offerings to God

Hezekiah charged the assembly of the people to offer sacrifices and thank offerings to God, and all the people did it with rejoicing over what God had prepared for them (vv. 31-36). This was a great restoration, a great revival.

B. Recovering the Passover

In 30:1—31:1 we see that Hezekiah recovered the Passover. The Passover had been lost, and the people no longer kept it, but Hezekiah recovered it.

1. The Degraded Children of Israel
Not Holding the Passover for a Long Time

The degraded children of Israel had not held the Passover for a long time as it was decreed in Moses' writing (30:5b).

2. Hezekiah Recovering the Passover
by Sending Letters to All Israel and Judah

Hezekiah recovered the Passover by sending letters to all Israel and Judah telling them to come to Jerusalem to hold the Passover of Jehovah (vv. 1-12).

a. Trying to Keep the Oneness of All God's Elect

He sent letters not only to the people of Judah but to all the people of Israel in order to keep the oneness of all God's elect (vv. 1a, 6a). By that time God's elect people had been divided. Hezekiah tried to unite them by inviting them all to keep the Passover.

b. Asking All the People of Israel and Judah
to Come to Jerusalem Where the House of God Was

Hezekiah asked all the people of Israel and Judah to come to Jerusalem where the house of God was to hold the Passover in order to remind them to keep the one unique ground of the worship of God among all Israel (v. 1b; cf. Deut. 12:5, 11, 13-14). He realized that keeping the unique ground pleases the heart of God.

c. Some Men from Asher, Manasseh, and Zebulun
Humbling Themselves and Coming to Jerusalem

The divisive people of Ephraim and Manasseh and as far as Zebulun laughed the runners of the letters to scorn and mocked them, but some men from Asher, Manasseh, and Zebulun humbled themselves and came to Jerusalem (2 Chron. 30:10-11). This is a type of today's situation. If we invite some denominational people to come to worship God on the church ground, they might know that this would be right, but they might not humble themselves and come to the proper ground, for this would cause them to lose face.

d. The Hand of God Being upon the People of Judah

Moreover, the hand of God was on the people of Judah, giving them one heart to perform the commandment of Hezekiah and the officers according to the word of Jehovah (v. 12). They listened to Hezekiah and the leaders, and then they took action according to God's word, according to God's revelation.

3. A Very Great Assembly Gathering at Jerusalem to Hold the Feast of Unleavened Bread

A very great assembly gathered at Jerusalem to hold the Feast of Unleavened Bread in the second month (vv. 13-22). The Feast of Unleavened Bread, which lasted seven days, was a continuation of the Passover, which lasted only one day.

a. Removing the Idolatrous Altars in Jerusalem

They removed the idolatrous altars that were in Jerusalem and they removed all the incense altars and threw them into the brook Kidron (v. 14). Everywhere in Jerusalem altars had been built for the idols, but Hezekiah and those who had gathered at Jerusalem to hold the Feast of Unleavened Bread cleared them away.

b. The Priests, the Levites, and the People Sanctifying Themselves unto God

The priests, the Levites, and the people sanctified themselves to God (vv. 15-17). The priests and the Levites brought burnt offerings to the house of Jehovah, and the Levites offered sacrifices for those who were not clean, to sanctify them to Jehovah.

c. Hezekiah Praying for Many from Ephraim, Manasseh, Issachar, and Zebulun

Hezekiah prayed for many from Ephraim, Manasseh, Issachar, and Zebulun who ate the Passover yet had not cleansed themselves. God heard Hezekiah and healed the people (vv. 18-20; cf. 1 Cor. 11:30-31). Some who ate the Passover had not cleansed themselves, and they got sick as a result. This is also a type. Once again we see that certain details of the New Testament economy are clearly portrayed in the Old Testament types.

d. The Children of Israel at Jerusalem Holding the Feast of Unleavened Bread with Great Rejoicing and Praising

The children of Israel at Jerusalem held the Feast of Unleavened Bread for seven days with great rejoicing and praising, and they repeated it with joy for another seven days (2 Chron. 30:21-26). Have you ever enjoyed the Lord's table so much on the Lord's Day that you had the Lord's table again the next day? How good that would be! After the people repeated the Feast of Unleavened Bread for another seven days, the priests and the Levites blessed the people, and their voice was heard and their prayer went up to God's sanctuary, to heaven (v. 27).

4. All Israel in the Cities of Judah Going Out to Smash the Pillars, Hew Down the Asherim, and Pull Down the High Places and the Altars

When all this was finished, all Israel in the cities of Judah went out to smash the pillars, hew down the Asherim, and pull down the high places and the altars out of all Judah, Benjamin, Ephraim, and Manasseh (31:1). In doing this, Hezekiah was surely pleasing to God.

C. Setting the Services of the Priests and the Levites in Order

In 31:2-21 Hezekiah set the services of the priests and the Levites in order. This signifies Christ, as the Head, setting in order the services of God in the church.

1. Appointing the Divisions of the Priests and the Levites

Hezekiah appointed the divisions of the priests and the Levites by their divisions for the offerings and praise in the gates of the temple of Jehovah (v. 2).

2. Appointing His Portion of His Substance for the Burnt Offerings

Hezekiah appointed his portion of his substance for the burnt offerings, the morning and evening burnt offerings and the burnt offerings of the Sabbath, the new moon, and the appointed feasts (v. 3). This indicates that he offered much of his substance to God.

3. Commanding the People Who Dwelt in Jerusalem to Give the Portion for the Priests and the Levites

Hezekiah commanded the people who dwelt in Jerusalem to give the portion for the priests and the Levites (v. 4), thereby supporting the priests and the Levites according to their daily necessities. This indicates that prior to this time, the need of the priests and the Levites had been neglected. The children of Israel gave in abundance for the priests and the Levites in distribution according to their divisions (vv. 5-19). The people took the responsibility of supporting the priests and the Levites.

4. Doing What Was Good, Upright, and Faithful before Jehovah His God with All His Heart

What Hezekiah did in verses 4 through 19 he did throughout all Judah. He did what was good, upright, and faithful before Jehovah his God with all his heart, and he prospered (vv. 20-21). He was the kind of person who should prosper.

D. Building a Defense against the Invasion of the Assyrians, Trusting in God, and Encouraging His People to Do So

Hezekiah built a defense against the invasion of the Assyrians (32:1-5). He trusted in God and encouraged his people to do so by saying, "Be strong and be bold; do not be afraid or dismayed because of the king of Assyria or because of all the multitude that is with him, for there is Someone greater with us than with him: with him is an arm of flesh, but with us is Jehovah our God to help us and to fight our battles" (vv. 6-8a). Here we see Hezekiah's faith, his trust in Jehovah. Here we also see that the people relied on the words of Hezekiah king of Judah (v. 8b).

However, not even Hezekiah was perfect. Here in 2 Chronicles there is no mention of Hezekiah's shortcomings, but within him there was something for his own interest and desire. This is clearly revealed in 2 Kings 20:1-19 and Isaiah 38 and 39.

XI. OF MANASSEH

In 2 Chronicles 33:11-17 we have a word concerning Manasseh. He was the son of Hezekiah and he reigned for fifty-five years.

A. Being Disciplined by Jehovah

Manasseh was disciplined by Jehovah and was captured by the Assyrians and taken to Babylon (v. 11).

B. Entreating Jehovah His God and Humbling Himself Greatly before the God of His Fathers

Manasseh entreated Jehovah his God in his distress, humbled himself greatly before the God of his fathers, and prayed to Him. God heard his supplication and brought him back to Jerusalem to his kingdom. Then he knew that Jehovah indeed was God (vv. 12-13). He came to know this through God's discipline.

C. Fortifying the City of David

Manasseh fortified the city of David (Bethlehem) and put the valorous captains in all the fortified cities in Judah (v. 14).

D. Removing the Foreign Gods and the Idol from the House of Jehovah

Manasseh removed the foreign gods and the idol from the house of Jehovah and all the altars that he had built on the mount of the house of Jehovah and in Jerusalem and cast them out of the city (v. 15). This indicates that, having repented, he cleared away all the impurity from the holy place.

E. Restoring the Altar of Jehovah
and Sacrificing on It

Manasseh restored the altar of Jehovah and sacrificed on it sacrifices of peace offerings and thank offerings. Also, he commanded Judah to serve Jehovah, the God of Israel (vv. 16-17). From this we see that although Manasseh had a bad beginning, he had a good ending.

XII. OF JOSIAH

In 34:3-7 there is a word concerning Josiah the grandson of Manasseh.

A. Beginning to Seek After
the God of David His Father

In the eighth year of his reign, while he was still young, Josiah began to seek after the God of David his father (v. 3a). He was only eight years of age when he became king, and in the eighth year of his reign he began to seek after God. This indicates that man has the capacity to contact God at a young age.

B. Beginning to Purge Judah and Jerusalem
of the High Places, the Asherim, the Idols,
and the Molten Images

In the twelfth year Josiah began to purge Judah and Jerusalem of the high places, the Asherim, the idols, and the molten images. The people tore down the altars to the Baals in his presence, and he hewed down the incense altars and ground the Asherim, the idols, and the molten images to dust and scattered it upon the graves of those who had sacrificed to them. Then he burned the bones of the priests upon their own altars (vv. 3b-5).

C. Tearing Down the Altars
throughout the Land of Israel

Throughout the land of Israel, Josiah, who was the king only of Judah, tore down the altars, beat the Asherim and

the idols into dust, and hewed down all the incense altars
(vv. 6-7).

XIII. THE DURATION OF THE CAPTIVITY OF ISRAEL AND THE PROCLAMATION OF THEIR RELEASE BY CYRUS

Second Chronicles 36:20b-23 speaks of the duration of the
captivity of Israel and the proclamation of their release by
Cyrus.

A. The Children of Israel Becoming Servants to the Kings of Babylon for Seventy Years

The children of Israel became servants to the kings of
Babylon for seventy years, until the reign of the kingdom
of Persia, so as to fulfill the word of Jehovah by the mouth of
Jeremiah (vv. 20b-21).

B. Cyrus Making a Proclamation for Israel's Return to Jerusalem to Build the Temple of God

In the first year of Cyrus king of Persia, Jehovah stirred
up the spirit of Cyrus king of Persia to make a proclamation
throughout all his kingdom for Israel's return to Jerusalem to
build the temple of God (vv. 22-23; Ezra 1:1-3).

MESSAGE ELEVEN

LIVING CHRIST FOR THE EXPRESSION OF GOD

Scripture Reading: Exo. 20:1-17; 25:16; Col. 1:15; Rom. 8:4; Phil. 1:19-21a

In this message I would like to give a word on the law as the testimony of God and as a type of Christ and on how the law is linked to God's New Testament economy.

THE LAW OF GOD

The examples of the kings of Judah show that God needed a people on the earth so that He could be incarnated in humanity. God also needed a land for His people that He might form a nation to set up His testimony. This testimony was set up according to the law of God.

We need to know what the law of God is. Some fundamental Christians may say the law of God consists mainly of the Ten Commandments (Exo. 20:1-17), that is, the moral law. However, the Ten Commandments with their statutes and ordinances occupy only a few chapters, Exodus 20—24. However, the law of God occupies not only these chapters but all the chapters from Exodus 20 to the end of Leviticus. Then what is the rest of God's law? The rest of God's law is the ceremonial law. From this we see that the law of God comprises the moral law (Exo. 20—24) and the ceremonial law (Exo. 25—Lev. 27).

THE MORAL LAW

The moral law includes the Ten Commandments with their statutes and ordinances. The first five commandments deal with our relationship with God and with our parents. The first three commandments are directly concerned with God; the fourth concerns God's Sabbath day; and the fifth

concerns our parents. Then the last five of the Ten Commandments deal with our relationship with one another. These are
the commandments not to murder, not to commit adultery,
not to steal, not to bear false witness against others, and not
to covet. These commandments, or laws, are brief, but they
cover almost everything concerning our relationship with one
another.

Eventually, the moral law, the Ten Commandments, became
the base of the civil law of many nations. For instance, Roman
law, which has been copied around the world, was based on
the last five of the Ten Commandments.

THE COMMANDMENT REGARDING COVETING
DEALING WITH AN INWARD MATTER

Let us consider the commandment regarding coveting. In
Philippians 3:6 Paul says that as to the righteousness which
is in the law, he was blameless. But in Romans 7 he admitted
that he was unable to keep the commandment regarding
coveting. "Neither did I know coveting, except the law had
said, 'You shall not covet.' But sin, seizing the opportunity
through the commandment, worked out in me coveting of
every kind" (vv. 7b-8a). Paul could keep the commandments
about murder, adultery, stealing, and bearing false witness,
for these four things are matters of outward conduct. The
commandment about coveting, however, deals with an inward
matter, and Paul could not keep himself from coveting.

Can you say that you have never coveted anything? When
you were a student, you might have seen someone with a nice
pen, and immediately you coveted that pen, desiring to
have it. Even in our family life we may covet certain things.
Suppose the members of a large family are having dessert
after dinner. Each of the children is given a piece of cheesecake. One of the children may look at the cheesecake given to
others and then complain that his piece is too small and ask
why he was not given a bigger piece. This is coveting. None of
us can say that we have never coveted anything.

THE LAW BEING A PORTRAIT OF GOD

The Ten Commandments were called the testimony of God

(Exo. 25:16). As the testimony of God the Ten Commandments are a picture, a portrait, of God. We may say that the law is a photograph of God.

A particular law is always a portrait of the person who makes that law. For example, if bank robbers could make laws, they surely would set up laws to make it legal to rob banks. Likewise, if evil people are elected to the United States Senate, they will make evil, sinful laws. The evil laws they make would be a portrait of the evil persons they are. On the contrary, good people establish good laws.

The law of God is a portrait of God. After a careful study of the last five of the Ten Commandments, we have seen that these five commandments are based on four of God's divine attributes: love, light, holiness, and righteousness. These attributes are the base upon which God's law was established. The more we consider the law of God, the more we realize that this lawmaker, this legislator, must be One who is full of love and light, One who is holy and righteous.

Because the law is God's portrait, God's image, it is called God's testimony. The ark in which the law was placed was called the ark of the testimony (Exo. 25:22).

THE LAW BEING A TYPE OF CHRIST

Based upon the fact that the law is the testimony of God, a picture of God, we may say that the law is also a type of Christ. How can the law be a type of Christ? The law is a type of Christ because Christ is God's portrait, God's picture, God's image (Col. 1:15).

THE LAW BEING LINKED TO GOD'S ECONOMY

Now we need to see how the law is linked to God's economy. In studying the books of history in the Old Testament, we need to learn how to link these books to God's economy. In His economy God chose Israel, established them as a people, formed them as a nation, and gave them the law. How can we link this with God's economy? God's economy is God becoming a man that man may become God in life and in nature (but not in the Godhead) to produce the organic Body of Christ, which will consummate in the New Jerusalem. Christ is the center, the reality, and the goal of God's economy. The law seems to have nothing to do with such an economy. How, then, can the law be linked to God's economy? The law is linked to God's economy because the law was given as God's portrait, God's picture, God's image, and God's testimony. As God's testimony the law is a type of Christ, who, being the image of God, is God's portrait, God's picture, God's testimony.

TO KEEP THE LAW BEING TO EXPRESS GOD

God charged Israel to keep the law. In typology, to keep the law means to express God. Keeping the law by not killing, not committing adultery, not stealing, not lying, and not coveting is the living of a God-man. Those who have the living of a God-man bear the image of God. They are a portrait of God and even a duplication of God.

The situation of today's world is utterly different from this. In the world we see not the life of a God-man but murder, adultery, fornication, stealing, lying, and coveting. Who tells the truth today? It is common for people to lie in a court of law in order to get money and then to boast about their lying. Many compete with others in business or at school because of their coveting. All the competitive ones are covetous. Some will even kill to get what they covet. Therefore, instead of being full of God-men, the earth is full of "scorpions."

LIVING THE LIFE OF A GOD-MAN
IN OUR MARRIED LIFE AND IN THE CHURCH LIFE

Let us now consider the situation in the recovery. We all are believers. We believe in the Lord Jesus. We have repented and come back to the Lord, and we have been saved, even dynamically saved. Yet in our daily life we may not have the living of a God-man.

We have pointed out that for the children of Israel to keep the law was to live God and express God. However, they did not keep the law, and therefore they did not live God and express God. The situation is the same with us today. For the most part, we do not express God in our daily living.

We need to have a God-man living in our married life. If a married brother would live the life of a God-man in his married life, he would surely be a good husband, for he would be a real God-man in loving his wife. Likewise, if a married sister would live the life of a God-man in her married life, she would be a good wife, submitting herself to her husband. We also need to have a God-man living in the church life, especially in relation to what we call the vital groups. How can we have a vital group if we ourselves are not vital? This is impossible. Suppose at dinner a brother and his wife are not happy with each other. They even exchange words and argue for quite a long time. Suddenly they remember that later that evening they must attend a meeting of their vital group. But how could this couple be vital in the meeting? Because they are not vital at home in their married life, they have no way to be vital in the meeting.

OUR NEED FOR A REAL REVIVAL

Because we are short of the God-man living, we need a real revival. The children of Israel had only an outward law, but today we have something much stronger and much higher than the law. We have the all-inclusive, life-giving, compounded, consummated Spirit in us, who is the bountiful supply of the Spirit of Jesus Christ (Phil. 1:19). We need to live Christ by the bountiful supply of the Spirit of Jesus Christ (vv. 20-21a).

We have such a Spirit within us, but what do we live and how do we live? Do we live Christ? In the church meetings we may live Christ, but do we live Christ at home with our husband or wife and with our children? We need a real revival to be God-men who live a life of always denying ourselves and being crucified to live Christ for the expression of God.

LIFE-STUDY OF FIRST AND SECOND CHRONICLES

MESSAGE TWELVE

A CONCLUDING WORD TO THE SUPPLEMENT TO THE HISTORY OF THE KINGS OF JUDAH

Scripture Reading: Heb. 4:12; 5:12-14

In this message we will give a concluding word to the supplement to the history of the kings of Judah.

I. COVERING ONLY THE KINGS OF THE KINGDOM OF JUDAH

The supplement in 1 and 2 Chronicles to the history of the kings covers only the kings of the kingdom of Judah and not one king of the kingdom of Israel.

II. REMAINING ON THE GROUND OF THE UNITY OF GOD'S CHOSEN PEOPLE

Unlike the kings of Israel, the kings of Judah remained on the ground of the unity of God's chosen people (Jerusalem) and kept the oneness according to the fundamental teaching of Moses.

Both the people of Judah and the people of Israel were the people of God. However, the people of Israel forsook God and made themselves the same as the people of mankind. As the elect of God Israel should have been sanctified, separated, unto the holy God. But the people of Israel, especially the kings, forsook God, turned to the idols, and set up centers of worship other than Jerusalem. That offended God to the uttermost. Israel was like a wife who forsakes her husband for another man. God, the Husband of His people, would never tolerate such a thing.

The kings of Judah remained on the ground chosen by God and stayed with God. In this matter God was happy with them. Although the condition of the kings of Judah was not pleasing to God, He was pleased with their standing on the proper ground and with their keeping of the fundamental faith according to God's word released to them through Moses. Because of their standing, God still had a people on earth who stood with Him and who at least tried to keep His word.

III. THEIR CONDITION NOT MATCHING THEIR STANDING

The condition of the kings of Judah did not match their standing on the unique ground and their fundamental belief. Most of these kings were wrong in their intention, purpose, desire, and preference.

To some extent this may also be the situation in some places in the recovery today. Certain ones take the proper ground and keep the fundamental faith, yet they live in the flesh, in the self, and in the natural man. They may be selfish and pursue their own interest, seeking glory and exaltation. Even worse, they may have ambition, something that is hateful and abominable in the sight of God. The root of every rebellion that took place among us in the past seventy-two years has been this ugly and evil matter of ambition.

IV. MOST OF THEM FORSAKING GOD AS THE FOUNTAIN OF LIVING WATERS AND FOLLOWING THE IDOLS

Most of the kings of Judah, like the kings of the kingdom of Israel, forsook God as the fountain of living waters and followed the idols to hew out for themselves broken cisterns which hold no water (Jer. 2:13). In principle, certain local churches have fallen somewhat into this kind of situation, forsaking the fountain of the living waters and following something else.

V. NONE OF THEM SEEMING TO HAVE A HEART THAT WAS ABSOLUTELY PURE IN SEEKING THE KINGDOM OF GOD

It seemed that none of the kings of Judah had a heart that was absolutely pure in seeking the kingdom of God, not their monarchy, and in establishing and living for the kingdom of God on the earth and not laboring and struggling for a monarchy for themselves and for their descendants. This is a picture of the situation in some so-called local churches.

VI. BREAKING THE LAW OF GOD

The kings of Judah broke the law of God, which was given to them through Moses to govern them and keep them in the enjoyment of the God-promised good land. God not only gave His elect people the good land and transferred them out of Egypt and into this land; God also gave them the law to govern them and keep them in the enjoyment of the good land. However, the kings of Judah broke the law of God.

VII. THE LAW OF GOD, WHICH WAS DECREED THROUGH MOSES, HAVING TWO SECTIONS

The law of God, which was decreed through Moses in the second part of Exodus, beginning from chapter twenty, and the entire book of Leviticus, had two sections—the moral section and the ceremonial section.

A. The Moral Section

The moral section (Exo. 20—24) was composed mainly of the Ten Commandments. The first five commandments governed the relationship of God's people with Him and their parents. The commandment regarding the honoring of parents was therefore ranked with the commandments which concerned their relationship with God. The last five commandments governed the relationship of God's people among themselves.

B. The Ceremonial Section

The ceremonial section (Exo. 25—Lev. 27) was composed of the laws of the tabernacle, the offerings, the priesthood, and the feasts. These four things are all types of Christ.

1. The Laws of the Tabernacle

The tabernacle typifies Christ as the embodiment of God (Col. 2:9; John 1:14) for God's people to contact Him and to enter into Him for their enjoyment. Christ has become a tabernacle, a dwelling place, which we can enter. This means that we can enter into Christ. Perhaps we need to practice saying, "Brother, let us enter into Christ. Let us go together into Christ and stay in Him." To remain in Christ is to enjoy God in Christ as the tabernacle.

2. The Laws of the Offerings

The offerings typify Christ as all kinds of sacrifices (Heb. 10:5-12) to meet the need of God toward His people and the need of His people before Him.

3. The Laws of the Priesthood

The priesthood typifies Christ as the High Priest (Heb. 8:1) taking care of God's chosen people before God.

4. The Laws of the Feasts

The feasts typify Christ as the bountiful enjoyment in every aspect assigned by God to His chosen people (Col. 2:16-17; Phil. 1:19).

The law of God is the portrait, the photograph, of God. Human laws always are a picture of the people who make them. This is true of the laws of every country. This is true even in your family life. The laws and regulations you make at home are your picture. The principle is the same with the law of God as a portrait of God. God's law portrays what kind of God He is.

I appreciate the commandments about not killing, not committing adultery, not stealing, not lying, and not coveting. How good it would be if everyone on earth kept these commandments! Suppose in the whole world there were no killing, no adultery, no stealing, no lying, and no coveting. If you took away these five things, the earth would be like heaven. However, everywhere people are killing, committing adultery, stealing, lying, and coveting.

God's people, His elect Israel, should have been different from mankind. They should have been a testimony of God, that is, the expression of God. If they had lived according to the law of God, they would have been the expression of God, for to keep the law is to express God. The kings of Judah stood on the ground chosen by God and they kept their belief in the Word of God, but they did not express God, because they did not keep the law of God. They did not live, conduct themselves, and have their being according to God's law. As the portrait of God and as the testimony of God, the law is a type of Christ. Christ is the end of the law (Rom. 10:4). He is the totality, the consummation, of the law. Since the law is the image of God, to keep the law is to bear the image of God and express God.

The kings of Judah stood on the proper ground and kept the fundamental faith, but they did not keep the law of God and thus they did not bear the image of God. They broke the law again and again, and this caused God to be angry with them. Eventually God came in to take them away from the good land. He would not allow them to enjoy the good land which He had given them, because they did not express Him but instead expressed His enemy, the devil.

Today Christ is the good land (Col. 1:12). We have been put into Christ; we have been transferred into Him. We need to stand on the proper ground and keep the proper faith as Paul did (2 Tim. 4:7). We also need to live and walk in Christ (Col. 2:6), conducting ourselves according to God to be His expression. Then we will enjoy Him, and the border of our enjoyment of Christ as the good land will be enlarged (1 Chron. 4:10).

VIII. GOD KNOWING THAT NO MAN CAN KEEP THE TEN COMMANDMENTS AS THE MORAL SECTION OF HIS LAW TO BE JUSTIFIED BY HIM

God knew that no man can keep the Ten Commandments as the moral section of His law to be justified by Him (Rom. 3:20). So, by His grace and according to His economy, He also gave His people the ceremonial section of His law, through which the condemned sinners, the breakers of the moral law of God, could contact Him and enter into Him to enjoy Him as their everything. In this way sinners could be justified by God to be righteous men (cf. Matt. 1:19a; Luke 1:6, 75; 2:25; 23:50). Foreknowing that we could not keep His commandments, God prepared the ceremonial law to be our salvation, to save us from the condemnation under the moral law.

IX. THE ENTIRE LAW OF GOD BEING DECREED WITH THE INTENTION OF EXPOSING AND CONVICTING HIS PEOPLE BY THE MORAL SECTION THAT THEY WOULD BE CONDUCTED TO THE CEREMONIAL SECTION

The entire law of God was decreed to His people by Him with the intention to expose and convict His people by the moral section of His law, that they would be conducted to the ceremonial section of His law, that is, conducted to the all-inclusive Christ as the embodiment of the Triune God for their redemption, salvation, and bountiful enjoyment in every aspect (Gal. 3:23-24) through all the ages unto eternity.

X. THE KINGS BREAKING THE ENTIRE LAW OF GOD AND PROVOKING THE WRATH OF GOD

Since the kings broke the entire law of God, both the moral and the ceremonial sections, again and again, they provoked the wrath of God and caused Him to give their good land to the Gentiles and make them captives to the pagan nations. Thus, they lost their portion in the enjoyment of the God-promised good land. This miserable outcome has lasted for twenty-seven centuries until today.

XI. TO STUDY THE HISTORY BOOKS OF THE OLD TESTAMENT IN THE WAY OF LIFE BEING TO COMPLY WITH GOD'S PURPOSE

To study the history books of the Old Testament in the way of life is to comply with God's purpose, that these books were written in His divine revelation for our admonition and enlightenment (1 Cor. 10:11).

LIFE-STUDY OF FIRST
AND SECOND CHRONICLES

MESSAGE THIRTEEN

THE RESEMBLANCE OF GOD AND MAN
IN THEIR IMAGES AND LIKENESSES

Scripture Reading: Gen. 1:26; 1 John 3:2b; Rev. 4:3a; 21:11b

In this message I would like to give a very brief word on the resemblance of God and man in their images and likenesses. We may think that we are very clear regarding this matter. Actually we may not be at all clear. Therefore, I would encourage you to study all the following points very carefully. As we consider these we may wonder whether man resembles God or God resembles man.

I. THERE BEING NO "MANKIND"
CREATED BY GOD IN HIS CREATION

There was no "mankind" created by God in His creation. Genesis 1 tells us that God created all the fish, the birds, the beasts, and the cattle after their kind (vv. 24-25). Although God created everything after its kind, God did not create "mankind." In God's creation there was not such a thing as "mankind."

II. GOD CREATING ADAM IN HIS OWN IMAGE

If God did not create "mankind," then after what kind was man created? Genesis 1:26 indicates that man is after God's kind. This verse says, "Let us [the Divine Trinity] make adam [Heb. *adam,* denoting red clay] in our image, after our likeness." Hence, what God made here was after His own kind, that is, God-kind. The word *man* is not used in the Hebrew text of Genesis 1:26. Here we are told that God created *adam,* which means "red clay." God created something of red clay in His own image and after His own likeness.

Having the image of God, this work of red clay looked like God. At least we can say that this clay was a figure of God, made after God's kind. Therefore, it was God-kind.

In Genesis 1:26 God created something according to Himself. What He made was a reproduction of Himself. If God had made ten thousand pieces of clay in His image and after His likeness, those ten thousand pieces of clay would all have been figures of God, the mass reproduction of God.

III. THREE MEN APPEARING TO ABRAHAM BEFORE CHRIST'S INCARNATION

In Genesis 18:2-13 three men appeared to Abraham. One of these men was Christ—Jehovah—and the other two were angels (19:1). The appearing of these three men to Abraham took place before Christ's incarnation. This means that two thousand years before His incarnation, God appeared as a man when He visited His friend Abraham. Abraham prepared water for Him to wash His feet, and Abraham's wife, Sarah, prepared a meal that this man ate. This is a mystery. When did Christ become a man—at the time of His incarnation or before the incarnation?

IV. THE ANGEL OF GOD APPEARING TO MANOAH AND HIS WIFE

The angel of God (God, Jehovah, a man of God—Christ) appeared to Manoah and his wife before Christ's incarnation (Judg. 13:3-6, 22-23).

V. A SON OF MAN COMING WITH THE CLOUDS OF HEAVEN

According to Daniel 7:13-14 Daniel saw a vision of a Son of Man coming with the clouds of heaven, and He came even to the Ancient of Days—the God of eternity—and they brought Him near before Him. There was given Him dominion, glory, and a kingdom that all the peoples, nations, and languages should serve Him. His dominion is an everlasting dominion, which shall not pass away, and His kingdom that which shall not be destroyed. Daniel saw such a vision of Christ as the Son of Man before Christ's incarnation.

VI. ADAM BEING A TYPE OF CHRIST

Adam was a type, a prefigure, of Christ (Rom. 5:14).

VII. CHRIST BEING THE IMAGE OF THE INVISIBLE GOD

The piece of red clay in Genesis 1:26 was a type of Christ, and Christ is the image of the invisible God (Col. 1:15).

VIII. THE WORD BECOMING FLESH

The Word (God) became flesh (John 1:14), becoming the flesh of sin only in its likeness (Rom. 8:3). God as the Word who became flesh had only the outward appearance of the flesh of sin, not the sinful nature of the flesh of sin.

IX. CHRIST TAKING THE FORM OF A SLAVE

Christ, who exists in the form of God, took the form of a slave, becoming in the likeness of men and being found in fashion as a man, in His incarnation (Phil. 2:6-8).

X. STEPHEN SEEING THE SON OF MAN AT THE RIGHT HAND OF GOD

Stephen saw the heavens opened up and the Son of Man—Christ—at the right hand of God (Acts 7:56). Stephen saw this after Christ's ascension to the heavens. This indicates that Christ is in the heavens still as the Son of Man. Concerning this, *Hymns,* #132 says:

> Lo! in heaven Jesus sitting,
> Christ the Lord is there enthroned;
> As the man by God exalted,
> With God's glory He is crowned.

XI. THE SON OF MAN COMING ON THE CLOUDS OF HEAVEN

In Matthew 26:64 the Lord Jesus said, "You will see the Son of Man sitting at the right hand of Power [God] and coming on the clouds of heaven." This refers to Christ's second coming. When the Lord Jesus comes back, He will still be the Son of Man.

XII. CONFORMED TO THE IMAGE OF GOD'S SON

In Romans 8:29 Paul tells us that those whom God foreknew, He also predestinated to be conformed to the image of His Son, that He might be the Firstborn among many brothers. This verse assures us that we, the believers in Christ, will all be conformed to the image of the Son of God.

XIII. BEING TRANSFORMED INTO THE SAME IMAGE

Second Corinthians 3:18 says, "We all with unveiled face, beholding and reflecting like a mirror the glory of the Lord, are being transformed into the same image from glory to glory, even as from the Lord Spirit." Romans 12:2a speaks of our being transformed by the renewing of the mind. He as God has done a lot to make Himself in the form and likeness of man. Now He intends to transform us into the same image and conform us to the image of the Son of God.

XIV. CHILDREN OF GOD WITHOUT BLEMISH

Philippians 2:15 speaks of our being blameless and guileless, children of God without blemish in the midst of a crooked and perverted generation, among whom we shine as luminaries in the world.

XV. THE LORD TRANSFIGURING THE BODY OF OUR HUMILIATION TO BE CONFORMED TO THE BODY OF HIS GLORY

The Lord Jesus Christ will transfigure the body of our humiliation to be conformed to the body of His glory, according to His operation by which He is able even to subject all things to Himself (Phil. 3:21). He has the power to transfigure our body in such a way that it will be conformed to the body of His glory.

XVI. WE BEING LIKE HIM

We know that if Christ is manifested, we will be like Him wholly, perfectly, and absolutely because we will see Him even as He is (1 John 3:2b).

XVII. GOD BEING LIKE A JASPER STONE

All this will consummate in the New Jerusalem. Revelation 4:3 says, "He [God] who was sitting was like a jasper stone." This tells us that the appearance of God, the One sitting on the throne, is like jasper.

XVIII. THE NEW JERUSALEM'S LIGHT BEING LIKE A JASPER STONE

According to Revelation 21 the New Jerusalem's light is like a most precious stone, like a jasper stone (v. 11b). The building work of its wall is jasper, and the first foundation of the wall is also jasper (vv. 18a, 19). The wall is jasper, the first foundation of the wall is jasper, the light of the city is jasper, and God on the throne is like jasper. Eventually God and man, man and God, all have the appearance of jasper. This is the conclusion of the Bible.

The consummation of the Bible is the New Jerusalem—divinity mingled with humanity. Divinity becomes the dwelling place of humanity, and humanity becomes the home of divinity. In this city the glory of God is manifested in man, brightly and splendidly. We will be there, and we are on the way. We are in the process of being made "a piece of God," to look the same as God—jasper.

LIFE-STUDY OF EZRA

MESSAGE ONE

THE NEED OF A RETURN FROM CAPTIVITY

Scripture Reading: 2 Chron. 36:14-23; Ezra 1:1-5

In this message we come to the last three books of history in the Old Testament—Ezra, Nehemiah, and Esther.

A BRIEF SURVEY OF THE HISTORY OF ISRAEL

I believe that in eternity past God determined that, after the confusion of Babel, He would choose a man by the name of Abraham. After calling Abraham God spent many years to train him. Eventually, Abraham produced a son, Isaac. Isaac had two sons—Esau, whom God hated, and Jacob, whom God loved (Mal. 1:2-3; Rom. 9:13). For many years Jacob was dealt with under God's hand. Jacob produced twelve sons, and these sons became the twelve tribes of Israel.

When God called Abraham out of Chaldea, the land of Babel, He promised to give him the good land, the land of Canaan (Gen. 12:1, 7), and He brought Abraham into this land. Abraham, therefore, was the first one of God's chosen people to enter into the good land. Later, the twelve tribes drifted away from the good land to Egypt, where they remained for hundreds of years (Exo. 12:40-41). During this time in Egypt, the twelve tribes of Israel became a nation of about two million people. They were usurped, enslaved, and persecuted by Pharaoh, king of Egypt. They cried out to God, and He sent Moses to deliver them out of that land of slavery into the good land. God brought the people of Israel to Mount Sinai to train them and to give them the covenant, the testament, which included both the moral law and the ceremonial law. In giving Israel the law, God's intention was that they would be a nation of priests.

When the people of Israel were about to enter into the land of Canaan, God charged them through Moses to slaughter all the Canaanites. He also charged them to destroy all the idols and everything related to idolatry. Joshua took this charge and he was faithful to it, but he was not faithful absolutely. Instead of slaughtering all the Canaanites, he allowed some to remain.

In the law given on Mount Sinai, God commanded the people of Israel concerning how to behave in relation to Him and in relation to one another. He did not want them to forsake Him, the fountain of living water, and hew out cisterns (idols) which are broken and which cannot retain water. He wanted them to love one another and not to murder, not to commit adultery, not to steal, not to lie, and not to covet. They were to take care of others, even returning lost things to their owner. This was the kind of life that was ordained by God. It was a heavenly life lived by earthly people. A people with such a living could surely be called the kingdom of God.

However, after Israel entered into the good land, they were not faithful to God. The people of Israel failed God and eventually were divided into the kingdom of Judah and the kingdom of Israel. The kingdom of Israel became apostate; they forsook God and set up other worship centers in addition to the unique center at Jerusalem. The kingdom of Israel was captured by the Assyrians, and later the kingdom of Judah was captured by the Babylonians. At that time the city of Jerusalem was captured and was not returned to Israel until 1967.

GOD GIVING UP THE PEOPLE OF ISRAEL TO CAPTIVITY AND PROMISING TO BRING THEM BACK FROM CAPTIVITY

At the end of 2 Chronicles, in God's eyes the condition and situation of Israel were miserable. The land was usurped and taken over by pagans, and the people of Israel were given by God as captives to the heathens. Furthermore, the temple was burned and the wall of Jerusalem was torn down. The entire good land, the so-called holy land, was devastated.

When Jeremiah saw all this, sitting on the top of Mount Zion and looking down at Jerusalem, he lamented bitterly. All the leading ones and all the noble ones of his countrymen had been taken away to captivity in Babylon, and only the poorest of the people were left to keep the land. It is no wonder that Jeremiah lamented. Eventually, he himself was taken captive to Egypt and there he was put to death. What a pitiful situation!

Such a condition lasted for seventy years, as Jeremiah himself had prophesied. While Jeremiah was lamenting, God came in to comfort him with the word that the captivity would not be forever but would last only seventy years (Jer. 25:11). God assured him that the miserable situation of his country and his people, of the temple and the city, would last for just seventy years. Some of the captured ones, such as Daniel, would still be alive at the expiration of the seventy years. When Zerubbabel led the first return from Babylon to Jerusalem, Daniel was still alive there in Babylon. Therefore, God comforted Jeremiah by assuring him that just as He gave the people up to captivity, He would also bring them back from their captivity. God would bring them back, not as captives but as triumphant warriors.

THE RETURN FROM CAPTIVITY
THROUGH THE SECRET PRESERVING CARE
OF THE HIDING GOD

Following 1 and 2 Chronicles, we have the books of Ezra, Nehemiah, and Esther. The book of Ezra is concerned with the return to Jerusalem to rebuild the temple, and the book of Nehemiah is concerned with the repair, the rebuilding, of the city. The book of Esther shows us how the omnipresent and omnipotent God became the hiding God in protecting His captured elect, who were scattered in their captivity.

Apparently God would not do anything for His people, for He is a God who hides Himself (Isa. 45:15). This is why in the book of Esther God is not referred to by any of His divine titles. In this book there is no explicit mention of God; the word *God* is not even used. Yet this book shows us that God is present in a hidden way, exercising His sovereignty in the wisest manner to preserve His elect. Because of this, His elect under the persecution in their captivity could survive and multiply, in order that one day they might be brought by God to their fathers' land.

The first group returned under Zerubbabel, a descendant of David, of the royal family. He was appointed the governor of Judah by Cyrus the king. The second group returned under Ezra, a priest and a scribe. As we have pointed out, this return was made possible through the secret preserving care of the hiding God in their captivity.

God let His people be captured and then scattered in their captivity. He also let the holy land be usurped and occupied, and He left the city of Jerusalem to lie waste. Seemingly the omnipotent and omnipresent God was not doing anything for the people of Israel. Actually He was protecting and preserving them in a hidden way.

The situation is the same today regarding the Middle East. The decision concerning Israel does not rest with the politicians and statesmen but with the hidden God. One day the omnipresent and omnipotent God will appear as the Son of Man, who will come back to take possession of the earth. He will place His right foot on the sea and His left on the land (Rev. 10:1-2), indicating that He has come to take possession of the earth and the sea. This One who is coming back to the earth is Jesus Christ, the God-man. When He comes, other God-men—the overcomers—will be with Him.

THE HISTORY OF THE PEOPLE OF ISRAEL BEING A TYPE OF THE NEW TESTAMENT BELIEVERS AS GOD'S ELECT

We need to remember that all the history of the people of Israel is a type, typifying the New Testament believers as God's elect. Israel, therefore, is a type of the church. The church was established by the Lord as the Head through His apostles in the first century. Yet by the end of the first century the church became degraded. This means that the church was captured.

Even among us, individually, whoever is defeated in the spiritual life has been captured. He will remain in captivity until he repents. Through his repentance he will be brought back. If we are captured, we are captured away from the enjoyment of Christ. But our repentance brings us back to Him, back to the enjoyment of Christ. Today we are in a situation that is typified by the situation at Ezra's time. Some of us have come back already, and others are still on the way.

OUR NEED TO BE CLEAR
CONCERNING THREE SITUATIONS

We all need to be clear concerning three situations: the world situation, the situation of Christianity, and our situation in the Lord's recovery. The worldly empires are the usurpers, and Christianity is our opposer. We in the Lord's recovery should not consider ourselves as nothing. We know the world situation, we know the situation of Christianity, and we know the hidden God.

I have the full peace that we are in the hand of the omnipresent and omnipotent yet hiding God, who is exercising His wise sovereignty to protect us, keep us, and save us. We do not need to worry about who will oppose us or who will persecute us. We have to believe in this hiding God. He is wise and He is sovereign. He can do everything under His wise sovereignty.

LIFE-STUDY OF EZRA

MESSAGE TWO

AN INTRODUCTORY WORD

Scripture Reading: Ezra 1:1-5

In this message we will give an introductory word to our life-study of Ezra.

I. EZRA, NEHEMIAH, AND ESTHER BEING THE LAST THREE BOOKS OF THE HISTORY OF GOD'S CHOSEN PEOPLE IN THE OLD TESTAMENT

Ezra, Nehemiah, and Esther are the last three books of the history of God's chosen people in the Old Testament after 1 and 2 Chronicles. These three books all are related to God's chosen people in their captivity. The first two cover in a public way the return of God's people from their captivity (cf. Daniel, Haggai, Zechariah, and Malachi), and the last one presents to us a pattern of how the hidden God, in a secret way, takes care of His chosen people in their captivity.

II. THE WRITER

The writer of the book of Ezra was Ezra, whose name means "help" or "helper." He was a descendant of Aaron (7:1-5), a priest and a scribe skilled in the law of Moses (vv. 6, 11-12). There are three Ezras in the Bible: one was a priest who returned with Zerubbabel (Neh. 12:1), one was a descendant of Caleb (1 Chron. 4:15-17), and one was the writer of this book.

III. THE TIME

Regarding the time of writing, the contents of this book cover a period of about eighty years, from 536-457 B.C.

IV. THE CONTENTS

It is very important for us to know the contents of the book of Ezra. This book gives us a record of the two returns of the children of Israel from their captivity. The first return was under Zerubbabel, a descendant of the royal family of David (chs. 1—6). Zerubbabel should have been the one to succeed the throne of David, but he was appointed to be the governor of Judah by Cyrus. The second return was under Ezra, a priest as the descendant of Aaron (chs. 7—10).

It is significant that Zerubbabel was of the royal tribe (Judah) and that Ezra was a descendant of a priestly family. The priests took care of God's speaking, and the kings took care of God's ruling. All that God has been doing is mainly in these two matters of speaking and ruling.

V. THE CRUCIAL POINTS

The book of Ezra stresses the return of the children of Israel from their captivity. This return is crucial in four points.

A. The Return of the Children of Israel from Their Captivity Recovering the Purpose of God's Calling of Them

The children of Israel were called by God and separated by God unto Himself as His testimony. Their captivity had annulled this purpose. The return of the children of Israel from their captivity recovered the purpose of God's calling of them.

As a people, the children of Israel were supposed to be a testimony of God. In what way was Israel to be a testimony to God? If we would answer this question, we need to see that the law given through Moses was called the testimony (Exo. 25:16, 21) because it is a portrait of God. As the Giver of the law, God is portrayed in the law according to what He is. In particular, the Ten Commandments are God's testimony. The ark was called the ark of the testimony (25:22; 26:33), and the tabernacle was called the tabernacle of testimony (Num. 1:50, 53).

The Ten Commandments, inscribed on two tablets of stone, are divided into two groups of five commandments, like the ten fingers on our two hands. Each group of five commandments is divided into four plus one. In the first group, the first three commandments are concerned with God and charge us not to have any god other than God, not to worship idols, and not to take the name of God in vain. God must be the unique God to us. The fourth commandment concerns the keeping of the Sabbath. The real significance of keeping the Sabbath is that we must stop ourselves in order to be one with God. Those who do not keep the Sabbath may gain a day for themselves, but they lose God. The commandment regarding the Sabbath is also related to God. Thus, the first four commandments are all concerned with God.

The fifth commandment, concerning honoring our parents, ranks our parents with God and points to God as our origin. Our origin is our parents, and the origin of our parents is God. When we honor our parents, we honor God. From this we see that honoring our parents is a very significant matter.

The second group of five commandments is concerned with our relationships one to another. These are the commandments not to kill, not to commit adultery, not to steal, not to lie, and not to covet. How wonderful our society would be if there were no killing, no adultery, no stealing, no lying, and no coveting. Our community would be a marvelous place if everyone was loving, pure, truthful, and helpful. A people who keep these last five commandments would surely be a real testimony of God, testifying that their God is the God of love, purity, sympathy, and truthfulness. Such a people would surely be God's particular people, God's elect, separated unto Him and sanctified to the uttermost.

After the man created by God became fallen, mankind fell lower and lower until, at Babel, they became rotten to the uttermost. God gave up the created race after Babel. Then He called Abraham and gave his descendants the law as the testimony of God. He expected that Abraham's descendants would be a people who had only Jehovah as their God, who rested with God in oneness, who honored their origin, and who loved one another in purity and honesty. Such a people would be the same as God in expression. They would be the many reproductions of God on earth testifying of the one God in heaven. This was God's purpose in calling the children of Israel and separating them to Himself. But the children of Israel failed God, breaking every one of the Ten Commandments and becoming the same as mankind.

The testimony of God is that we have one God and no other gods, that we stop ourselves in order to be one with God and to enjoy Him and have Him as everything, and that we honor Him as our origin, which is signified by our parents. Israel was carried away into captivity, and God lost such a testimony. They were called by God for the purpose of being His testimony, and their captivity annulled this purpose. But the return of the children of Israel from their captivity recovered the purpose of God's calling of them.

B. Their Return from Their Captivity
to the Unique Ground of Jerusalem
Recovering Their Oneness

In order to have one testimony, God always kept the children of Israel together in a narrow piece of land, not allowing them to become too great in number. They were a particular people in a particular place, and they were in oneness. But the captivity scattered them, some to Assyria, some to Egypt, and most of them to Babylon. This caused them to be divided and thus to lose their oneness as a people for God's testimony. Their return from their captivity to the unique ground of Jerusalem (Deut. 12:5, 11-14) recovered this oneness. However, as we will see, in their return elements of the captivity returned with them.

C. Their Return from Their Captivity
Recovering Their Enjoyment of the Portion
of the Good Land Promised by God

God brought the children of Israel into His promised good land through His redemption and salvation that they might partake of the good land and enjoy it as their portion in God's economy. Because of their failure, they lost this portion of the

good land in their captivity. Their return from their captivity
recovered their enjoyment of the portion of the good land
promised by God.

Those who are in today's denominations do not stress the
enjoyment of Christ, and the denominational people are not
taught, instructed, and directed to enjoy Christ. When I was
with the denominations, I did not have any enjoyment of
Christ. Only after I left the denominations did I begin to
enjoy Christ.

Those who are in captivity are away from the good land,
away from Christ. The Israelites who were captives in Babylon were away from the good land. Likewise, the Christians in
the denominations are kept away by many things from the
enjoyment of Christ. They have the name of Christ but not
the enjoyment of Christ. If they would have the enjoyment of
Christ, they must leave their captivity and come back to the
proper ground where Christ, the good land, is.

D. God's Intention to Have His House Built and His Kingdom Established on the Earth

God intended to have His house built and His kingdom
established on the earth through Israel's participation in and
enjoyment of the good land. There would have been no way to
accomplish this unless the children of Israel returned to the
good land from their captivity.

Where is God's house and His kingdom today? Satan, the
enemy of God, has usurped the earth. He has kept the earth
as his house and as his kingdom. This has caused a great
problem. Why does God need a people today? God needs a
people because He wants a house where He is the Father and
a kingdom where He is the King. The Lord needs His house
and His kingdom in order to carry out His eternal economy.
This is the reason God needs a return of His people from their
captivity. God needs a house and a kingdom, and for this He
needs the recovery.

All the foregoing crucial points are types typifying today's
recovery of the church life, which is a recovery out of the
church's captivity in the great Babylon (Rev. 17:1-6) back to
the unique ground of God's choice.

VI. THE SECTIONS

The book of Ezra has two sections: the return of the captivity under the kingly leadership of Zerubbabel (chs. 1—6) and the return of the captivity under the priestly leadership of Ezra (chs. 7—10).

LIFE-STUDY OF EZRA

MESSAGE THREE

THE RETURN OF THE CAPTIVITY
UNDER THE KINGLY LEADERSHIP OF ZERUBBABEL

Scripture Reading: Ezra 1—6

In this message we will consider the first return of the captivity, the return under the kingly leadership of Zerubbabel.

I. THE DECREE OF CYRUS KING OF PERSIA

The return of the captivity under the leadership of Zerubbabel was according to the decree of Cyrus king of Persia (Ezra 1:1-4; 2 Chron. 36:22-23).

A. In His First Year

Cyrus made this decree in his first year (Ezra 1:1a).

B. By God's Stirring Up of His Spirit

Cyrus made this decree because God stirred up his spirit (v. 1b). This stirring up was a work of the hiding God.

C. In Fulfillment of the Word of Jehovah by the Mouth of Jeremiah

This decree was a fulfillment of the word of Jehovah by the mouth of Jeremiah that Israel would return after the seventieth year of their captivity in Babylon (v. 1b).

D. Ordering the Captivity of Israel to Go Back to Jerusalem and Rebuild the House of God

In his decree Cyrus ordered the captives of Israel to go back to Jerusalem and rebuild the house of God there (vv. 2-4). Because Cyrus was such a person, in the book of

Isaiah he is considered a servant of God to fulfill God's purpose (Isa. 45:1-4, 13).

II. THE RESPONSE OF THE HEADS OF THE FATHERS' HOUSES OF JUDAH AND BENJAMIN, THE PRIESTS, AND THE LEVITES

In verses 5 and 6 we have a word concerning the response of the heads of the fathers' houses of Judah and Benjamin, the priests, and the Levites.

A. By God's Stirring Up of Their Spirit

Everyone whose spirit God had stirred up rose up to go up to build the house of Jehovah in Jerusalem (v. 5). This surely was God's move, for He stirred up the spirit of Cyrus to make the decree and then stirred up the spirits of all the leaders of the three tribes of Judah, Benjamin, and Levi.

B. All the Israelites around Them Strengthening Their Hands

All the Israelites around them strengthened their hands with their offerings of their precious vessels (v. 6).

III. THE COOPERATION OF KING CYRUS

In verses 7 through 11 we see the cooperation of King Cyrus. He cooperated by returning the 5,400 vessels of gold and silver of the house of Jehovah, captured by Nebuchadnezzar from Jerusalem and put in the house of his gods (vv. 7, 11). He handed over the vessels, by enumerating them to Sheshbazzar (Zerubbabel—2:2), the prince of Judah, to be brought back to Jerusalem for the house of God (1:8-11; 5:13-15).

IV. THE NUMBER OF THE RETURNED CAPTIVES

In 2:1-67 we have a clear and accurate record of the number of the captives who returned under Zerubbabel, the prince of Judah (1:8), the governor of the former kingdom of Judah (2:2, 63). Of the Judites, the Benjaminites, the priests, the Levites, the temple servants, and the children of Solomon's servants (vv. 3-58), the total number was 42,360, besides their male and female servants and the male and female singers (vv. 64-65). In addition, 652 common people and three houses of priests who could not give evidence of their fathers' houses were included with those who returned under Zerubbabel (vv. 59-63).

V. THE WILLING OFFERING OF SOME OF THE HEADS OF THE FATHERS' HOUSES

Verses 68 and 69 speak of the willing offering of some of the heads of the fathers' houses, after their arrival at the house of Jehovah in Jerusalem, for the house of Jehovah to restore it on its foundation. This means the heads of the fathers' houses willingly offered their precious things to God for the rebuilding of the temple.

VI. THE REBUILDING OF THE ALTAR OF GOD

Ezra 3:1-6a is concerned with the rebuilding of the altar of God.

A. In the Seventh Month

They rebuilt the altar in the seventh month of the year of their return (v. 1a).

B. The Children of Israel Gathering to Jerusalem as One Man

The children of Israel gathered from their cities to Jerusalem as one man (v. 1b). Not only the returned captives but also the Jews who had not been captured came to Jerusalem to rebuild the altar.

C. The Altar Being Built upon Its Bases

Joshua the high priest and his brothers the priests and Zerubbabel the governor and his brothers built the altar of the God of Israel upon its bases, as written in the law of Moses, the man of God. Then, for God's satisfaction, they offered burnt offerings on it to Jehovah, as written in the law of Moses (vv. 2-3). Here we see that they did everything according to God's word.

D. Keeping the Feast of Tabernacles

They kept the Feast of Tabernacles and offered the daily burnt offerings and the offerings of the new moons and of all the appointed feasts of Jehovah (vv. 4-6a). This indicates that they recovered the worship of God, which had been lost for at least seventy years.

VII. THE REBUILDING OF THE HOUSE OF GOD

In verses 6b through 13 we have a record of the rebuilding of the house of God.

A. Hiring Stone Hewers and Carpenters

They hired stone hewers and carpenters, and they supplied the Sidonians and the Tyrians the daily necessities for them to bring cedar trees from Lebanon to Joppa (v. 7).

B. In the Second Month of the Second Year after Their Return

In the second month of the second year after their return, they began to rebuild the house of God with praise to Jehovah by the priests (vv. 8-13). Many of the priests and Levites and heads of the fathers' houses, the old men who had seen the first house, the original temple of God, wept with a loud voice when the foundation of this house was laid, and many shouted aloud for joy (v. 12). The people could not discern the sound of the shout of joy from the sound of the weeping of the people (v. 13).

VIII. THE FRUSTRATION

Chapter four gives us an account of the frustration to the rebuilding of the house of God.

A. The Adversaries of Judah and Benjamin Pretending to Help the Rebuilding of the House of Jehovah

The adversaries of Judah and Benjamin, people brought from Babylon and Assyria by the king of Assyria to inhabit Samaria (2 Kings 17:24), who imitated Israel in seeking God and sacrificing to God, pretended to help the rebuilding of the house of Jehovah, but they were rejected by Zerubbabel, Joshua, and the rest of the heads of the fathers' houses. The enemies hired counselors to frustrate the rebuilding throughout all the days of Cyrus king of Persia until the reign of Darius king of Persia, and in the beginning of the reign of Ahasuerus they wrote an accusation against the inhabitants of Judah and Jerusalem (Ezra 4:1-6). This typifies that today when we come back to the recovery to build the house of God, some nearby ones would make proposals that are mostly frustrations. This is Satan's subtlety. In his time, Zerubbabel saw through these proposals and rejected them.

B. Artaxerxes Decreeing to Stop the Building of the House of God by Force and Power

In the days of Artaxerxes, a party of the inhabitants of Samaria and the rest of the lands beyond the River (maybe of the same adversaries in verse 1) wrote to Artaxerxes against Jerusalem. Artaxerxes decreed to stop the rebuilding of the house of God by force and power; and the work of the house of God ceased until the second year of the reign of Darius king of Persia (vv. 7-24).

IX. THE CONTINUAL REBUILDING WORK

The rebuilding work continued through the encouragement and help of the prophecies of the prophets Haggai and Zechariah (5:1-2).

X. THE CONFIRMATION OF THE DECREE OF DARIUS KING OF PERSIA

Ezra 5:3—6:12 tells us of the confirmation of the decree of Darius king of Persia. After the people stopped the work, they were encouraged by the prophets Haggai and Zechariah to continue the rebuilding work. At the same time this work was confirmed by the decree of Darius king of Persia.

A. The Rebuilding Questioned and Referred to Darius

The rebuilding was questioned and referred to Darius

king of Persia by Tattenai, the governor beyond the River
(that is, west of the Jordan) and his companions (vv. 3-17).

B. Darius's Checking of the Decree of Cyrus

In 6:1-12 we have Darius's checking of the decree of
Cyrus and his confirmation to encourage and speed up the
rebuilding. After being questioned about the rebuilding,
Darius checked and confirmed the decree of Cyrus, finding
out that Cyrus had issued a decree to release Israel from
captivity so that they could go back to Jerusalem to rebuild
the house of God. Darius confirmed that there was such a
record, and his confirmation encouraged and sped up the
rebuilding.

XI. THE COMPLETION OF THE REBUILDING
OF THE HOUSE OF GOD

Verses 13 through 15 describe the completion of the
rebuilding of the house of God.

A. In Prosperity

The rebuilding was completed in prosperity through
the prophesying of the prophets Haggai and Zechariah
(vv. 13-14).

B. On the Third Day of the Month Adar

The work of rebuilding the house of Jehovah was completed on the third day of the month Adar, in the sixth year of
the reign of Darius the king (v. 15).

XII. THE DEDICATION
OF THE REBUILT HOUSE OF GOD

Verses 16 through 18 speak of the dedication of the rebuilt
house of God.

A. With Joy

The dedication of the rebuilt house of God was with the
joy of the priests, the Levites, and the rest of the children
of the captivity in celebration (v. 16).

B. With the Offerings
for the Dedication and a Sin Offering

The dedication was also with the offerings for the dedication and a sin offering for all the tribes of Israel (v. 17). This indicates that as they were offering burnt offerings for God's satisfaction, they could not forget their sin and therefore offered a sin offering.

C. With the Setting Up of the Services
of the Priests and of the Levites

Finally, the rebuilt house was dedicated with the setting up of the services of the priests in their courses and of the Levites in their divisions, as written in the law of Moses (v. 18).

XIII. THE KEEPING OF THE PASSOVER
BY THE CHILDREN OF THE CAPTIVITY

The account of the return of the captivity under the kingly leadership of Zerubbabel concludes with the keeping of the Passover by the children of the captivity (vv. 19-22). The Passover was a most important matter.

A. Having Their Priests and Levites Purified

They kept the Passover by having their priests and Levites purified and themselves separated from the defilement of the nations in the good land (vv. 20-21).

B. Continuing with the Feast of Unleavened Bread

They continued with the Feast of Unleavened Bread for seven days with joy, for Jehovah had made them joyful and had turned the heart of the king of Assyria to them, to strengthen their hands in the work of the house of God (v. 22). The king of Assyria was Darius king of Persia, because Assyria was at that time a part of Persia.

Today very few believers care for the building up of a proper local church in their locality as the house of God. This means that God is kept homeless. He does have a home in the heavens with the angels, but He needs a home with the humanity of His heart's desire. God wants to have such a home.

We in the Lord's recovery do not like to see the saints scattered individually. The particular intention of the recovery is to have all the saints in the recovery come together in their localities to be built up together as the house of God in so many cities. Through such a house God will have His kingdom.

We need to have a desire to be freed from self and the natural life in order to be built up with others (see *Hymns*, #840). To be built we need to be adjusted, disciplined, corrected, and transformed. Then we will be able to come together to be built as the house of God in many localities.

LIFE-STUDY OF EZRA

THE RETURN OF THE CAPTIVITY
UNDER THE PRIESTLY LEADERSHIP OF EZRA

Scripture Reading: Ezra 7—10

For God to fulfill His promise, spoken through Jeremiah, that the captivity would last only for seventy years (Jer. 25:11-12; Dan. 9:2), He accomplished two returns. The first return was under the leadership of Zerubbabel, a royal descendant. The second return was under the leadership of Ezra, a priest.

The first return did not need the priestly leadership of Ezra; rather, it needed the kingly leadership of Zerubbabel, a royal descendant who knew how to govern. Zerubbabel governed quite well, taking the lead in building up the altar and the temple. After this, the need shifted from the royal family to the priesthood, to Ezra, a descendant of the high priest Aaron. Ezra was not only a priest but also a scribe, someone who was skilled in the law of God (Ezra 7:6). As such a person, Ezra had the capacity to meet the need.

I. THE RETURN OF THE CAPTIVITY UNDER EZRA

Chapters seven and eight are concerned with the return of the captivity under Ezra.

A. The Beginning of the Return
through the Request of Ezra to the King

The return of the captivity under Ezra began through his request to the king (7:1-10). Ezra must have appealed to the king to give many of the Jews in his empire the freedom to go back to the land of their fathers. As we will see, the king not only granted Ezra's request but also provided everything he needed.

1. Ezra's Genealogy

Ezra's genealogy in 7:1-5 indicates that he was a descendant of Aaron the chief priest.

2. The King's Granting of the Request of Ezra

The king granted the request of Ezra, a scribe skilled in the law of Moses (v. 6).

3. Coming Safely to Jerusalem

Ezra, some of the children of Israel, some of the priests, the Levites, the singers, the gatekeepers, and the temple servants left Babylon on the first day of the first month in the seventh year of Artaxerxes the king and came safely to Jerusalem on the first day of the fifth month according to the good hand of God.

The book of Ezra does not speak of the Spirit of God, but the hand of God is mentioned a number of times (7:6, 9, 28; 8:31). What is the difference between the Spirit of God and the hand of God? When God's Spirit works inwardly, that is the Spirit. When God's Spirit works outwardly, that is God's hand.

4. Ezra Having Set His Heart to Seek and Do the Law of Jehovah

Ezra had set his heart to seek and do the law of Jehovah and to teach His statutes and ordinances (7:10). We need to see the difference between the statutes and the ordinances. The Ten Commandments are the main items of the law, but all these commandments have their statutes, which give the details. For instance, the fourth commandment is about keeping the Sabbath. The details regarding this commandment are found in the statutes. The ordinances are statutes to which judgments have been added. When a judgment is added to a statute, that statute becomes an ordinance. Regarding the commandment to keep the Sabbath, there are not only statutes giving the details but also ordinances telling of the judgment that will come upon those who break this commandment. Ezra set his heart not only to seek and do the main part of the law of Jehovah but also to teach His statutes, the details, and His ordinances, the verdicts and judgments.

B. The Decree of Artaxerxes King of Persia

Verses 11 through 28 tell us about the decree of Artaxerxes king of Persia to Ezra the priest, the scribe.

1. Permitting the Children of Israel, the Priests, and the Levites to Go to Jerusalem

The king permitted the children of Israel, the priests, and the Levites to go to Jerusalem as they willed, with silver and gold and vessels (vv. 12-19). This means that they were permitted to go freely with all their wealth.

2. Permitting the Provision for the Needs of the House of God

The king also permitted the provision for the needs of the house of God out of the king's treasure house (v. 20).

3. Ordering All the Treasurers to Provide Whatever Ezra Required for the House of God

The king went on to order all the treasurers in the lands beyond the Great River, the Euphrates, to provide whatever Ezra the priest required for the house of God (vv. 21-23).

4. Ordering the Treasurers Not to Impose Tribute, Taxes, or Tolls

Next, the king ordered the treasurers not to impose tribute, taxes, or tolls on the priests, Levites, singers, gatekeepers, temple servants, or servants of this house of God (v. 24).

5. Authorizing Ezra to Appoint Magistrates and Judges

According to verses 25 and 26 the king authorized Ezra to appoint magistrates and judges to judge the people in the land, to teach them the laws of his God, and to execute judgment according to the law of God and the law of the king. Here the king did something for his own advantage. Without

a person such as Ezra, who would have been qualified to
maintain a proper order among the people in the good land?
In authorizing Ezra to appoint judges and magistrates, the
king of Persia was clever, for he knew that the ones appointed
by Ezra would execute judgment not only according to the
law of God but also according to the law of the king.

6. Ezra's Blessing to God

Verses 27 and 28 are Ezra's blessing to God. He blessed
God for putting such a thing as this into the king's heart to
beautify the house of Jehovah in Jerusalem, saying that God
had extended lovingkindness to him before the king, before
the king's counselors, and before all the mighty officers of the
king. Then Ezra declared that he was strengthened according
to the hand of Jehovah his God upon him. What the king did
for Ezra, he did according to the hand of Jehovah. To some
extent, the king, the counselors, and the mighty officers
might have realized that God was with the Jews. God's hand
was there, controlling everything sovereignly for the benefit
of His elect.

C. The Genealogical Enrollment

In 8:1-20 we have the genealogical enrollment of those
who returned from their captivity back to Jerusalem.

D. Ezra's Proclamation of a Fast

Ezra proclaimed a fast before they left Babylon, to humble
themselves before God to seek from Him a straight way for
them, rather than to ask for troops and horsemen from the
king to help them against the enemy in the way (vv. 21-23).
Instead of asking for troops, which the king would have
provided, Ezra put his trust in the good hand of God.

E. Ezra Setting Apart Twelve
of the Leading Men of the Priests

Ezra set apart twelve of the leading men of the priests
to take care of the offerings of silver, gold, and vessels for
the house of God and to bring them to the house of God in
Jerusalem (vv. 24-30). This was a serious responsibility, for

it involved risk and danger on the journey from Babylon to Jerusalem.

F. The Journey and Arrival of the Returned Captivity

Verses 31 through 34 describe the journey and arrival of the returned captivity.

1. Setting Out from the River Ahava

They set out from the river Ahava on the twelfth day of the first month, having the hand of their God upon them, who delivered them from the hand of the enemy and from people set in ambush on the way (v. 31).

2. Arriving at Jerusalem and Delivering All the Silver, Gold, and Vessels

They arrived at Jerusalem and delivered all the silver, gold, and vessels to the house of God by weighing them (vv. 32-34). This indicates that they delivered this wealth in a very careful way.

G. The Offerings to God by the Returned Captivity

Verse 35 speaks of the offerings to God by the returned captivity. As soon as they arrived, they offered burnt offerings and a sin offering.

H. The Returned Captivity's Delivering the King's Decrees

The returned captivity delivered the king's decrees to the king's satraps and to the governors of the provinces beyond the River, and these supported the people and the house of God (v. 36).

II. THE PURIFICATION OF THE RETURNED CAPTIVES FROM THE DEFILEMENT OF THE FOREIGN WIVES

Chapters nine and ten are an account of the purification of the returned captives from the defilement of the foreign wives. God had charged the children of Israel, when they entered into the good land, not to have intermarriage with

the peoples of the land. At Ezra's time, not only the common
people but even the priests and the Levites had foreign wives.

A. Initiated by the Officials
of the Returned Captives

This purification was initiated by the officials of the
returned captives (9:1-2). They accused the people of Israel,
the priests, and the Levites of not separating themselves from
the peoples of the lands but taking the daughters of the
nations for themselves and for their sons, thus mingling the
holy seed with the peoples of abominations. They accused
the leaders and the rulers of having been foremost in this
unfaithfulness to God.

B. Ezra's Reaction

Verses 3 through 15 describe Ezra's reaction.

1. Tearing His Garment

Ezra tore his garment and pulled out hair from his head
and his beard and sat down appalled with the gathering of
those who trembled at the words of the God of Israel (vv. 3-4).
Those who trembled at the words of God were the faithful
ones.

2. Making a Thorough Confession
of the Iniquities of the Children of Israel

Ezra then made a thorough confession of the iniquities of
the children of Israel from their forefathers' time to their
time, saying that their iniquities issued in the delivery of
their kings and their priests into the hand of the kings of the
lands and into captivity and shamefacedness (vv. 5-7).

3. Thanking God for Leaving
Them a Remnant to Escape

Ezra thanked God for leaving them a remnant to escape
and for giving them a peg in His holy place by extending His
lovingkindness to them in the sight of the kings of Persia
to give them a reviving, to raise up the house of their God,

and to give them a wall and to repair its ruins in Judah and Jerusalem (vv. 8-9).

4. Confessing Their Being Defiled

Ezra continued by confessing their being defiled with the uncleanness and abominations of the Canaanites in seeking their peace and prosperity, thus losing the right to enjoy the good of the promised land and to leave it for an inheritance to their children forever (vv. 10-15). Ezra was confessing that by taking foreign wives the people were despising and neglecting their right to enjoy the good land and as a result they were given by God into captivity.

C. The Congregation's Reaction

In 10:1-5 we have the congregation's reaction.

1. Weeping Very Bitterly
for Their Unfaithfulness against Their God

The people reacted by weeping very bitterly for their unfaithfulness against their God by marrying foreign women from the peoples of the land (vv. 1-2).

2. Making a Covenant with Their God

They also made a covenant with their God to put away all their foreign wives and those born of them, according to the counsel of Ezra and of those who trembled at the commandment of their God (v. 3).

3. Encouraging Ezra to Be Strong
and Bear His Responsibility

The people encouraged Ezra to be strong and bear his responsibility. Then they swore that they would do according to his word (vv. 4-5).

D. The Final Decision

Ezra 10:6-44 is a record of the final decision. A proclamation was made throughout Judah and Jerusalem to all the children of Israel to gather in Jerusalem within three days (vv. 6-9). Next, the decision was made to separate themselves

from the peoples of the land and from the foreign women
(vv. 10-14, 16-17). However, a few of the people stood up
against the decision, supported by one Levite (v. 15). Finally,
there was a list of all the men who had married foreign
women (vv. 18-44).

We have pointed out that Ezra emphasizes the matter of
God's hand. It was by His hand that God gave the children
of Israel into captivity. It was also by His hand that God
brought the children of Israel back from their captivity to
the land of their forefathers. Here we see that the same God
did two different things: He gave His people to their enemy as
captives and He delivered them from captivity and brought
them back to their fatherland. Ezra, a wise man, was clear
about this.

Ezra realized that the first return was not perfect, not
complete. He realized that there was the need for someone
who was skilled in the law of God to help the people to know
God not merely in a general way but according to what God
had spoken. Ezra had such a capacity, so he volunteered
himself to go to the king and to request a decree from the
king permitting the Jews to do everything freely.

Chapter one of Ezra tells us that God stirred up the spirit
of Cyrus king of Persia to make a proclamation concerning
the rebuilding of the house of God (vv. 1-2) and that He also
stirred up the spirit of the heads of the fathers' houses of
Judah and Benjamin, the priests, and the Levites to go up to
build the house of God in Jerusalem (v. 5). God was hiding
Himself, but at the expiration of the seventy years, He came
in to stir up the spirit of Cyrus. Cyrus must have been happy
that the great empire of Babylon was in his hand, and
regarding the Jews he might have wanted to do something
that was opposite to what the Babylonians had done.
Humanly speaking, Cyrus took the initiative to make the
decree. Actually, this was initiated by God in a hidden way.
Therefore, the first return from Babylon to Jerusalem was
initiated by God.

The second return was initiated by Ezra, a priest and a
scribe skilled in the Word of God. Ezra came to the king and
appealed to him to grant his request (7:6). From this we see

that sometimes God personally stirs us up in our spirit to do something for Him. However, often God is quiet, realizing that it is better that we do something because we have the capacity, as Ezra had. In this kind of situation, God is responsible for the things we do. Whether the things are stirred up by Him or stirred up by us, He will be in them, stretching out His hand to do everything to help us.

LIFE-STUDY OF EZRA

THE NEED FOR EZRAS—
THOSE SKILLED IN THE WORD OF GOD

Scripture Reading: Ezra 7:6, 10; 1:7-11

The Bible is unique, and everything contained in it is significant. At the very beginning, the Bible tells us that God created Adam as a creature in His kind (Gen. 1:26). Adam was God's kind only in likeness and appearance, not in life, nature, and constitution. God's desire was that Adam would be His kind not only in likeness but also in life, nature, and constitution.

GOD'S INTENTION THAT ISRAEL
WOULD BE HIS TESTIMONY

In Genesis 3:15 God promised that He would come to be the seed of woman. Later, He prophesied further He would come to be a seed of Abraham, which would be the blessing to all the nations (22:18). Eventually, God Himself was incarnated to be a man. However, God first, through His continuous labor, took more than one thousand years to produce and form the nation of Israel as a great type.

God selected Abraham, whose descendants fell into Egypt. God sent Moses to them to deliver them out of Egypt as a great nation, numbering about two million, and brought them to Mount Sinai, where they stayed for nearly a year to be educated by God. God's intention was to have Israel as His testimony, but according to their Egyptian culture they were a testimony of Egypt. For this reason God kept them at Mount Sinai to give them the Ten Commandments, all the statutes for the Ten Commandments, all the ordinances for the statutes, the tabernacle with all the furniture and all the offerings, the priesthood, and all the feasts, in order to build them up with a heavenly, divine constitution instead of an Egyptian constitution.

THE NATION OF ISRAEL BEING GOD-MEN IN TYPOLOGY BUT EVENTUALLY BECOMING DEGRADED

As a result of this time of education and training, the nation of Israel became an army not only formed and organized but also constituted to be God with man and man with God. Hence, in typology the Israelites were God-men. They were God-men, and everything related to them, even their environment with the pillar of cloud in the day and the pillar of fire at night, was God's expression. Their going forth became God's going forth (Psa. 68).

After a short time, however, the children of Israel no longer expressed God, and He let them die in the wilderness. Then God raised up the second generation, and they crossed the river Jordan by a great miracle. As a heavenly constituted army they came to Jericho. When they shouted, the city of Jericho fell. This was God's testimony. This was the move, the living, of God-men; it was God marching on. But when they came to the city of Ai, one among them caused them to fail. From that time onward, there was nothing among the Israelites but degradation. God sent the prophets to warn them and bring them back, but they refused to go along with God. Eventually, God brought in the Babylonians to possess the good land and carry the people of Israel away to Babylon to be disciplined and punished.

THE RETURN OF GOD'S PEOPLE UNDER ZERUBBABEL

God could not forget the good land, the promised land, the land of Immanuel (Isa. 8:8). The good land should be the land of God-men for the testimony of God. First, there was a return under the leadership of Zerubbabel, a descendant of the royal family. It was fitting for him to take the lead in the first return from captivity, because he had the capacity to administrate and to govern. He was a strong governor and he led the people in rebuilding the temple with the altar.

THE NEED FOR AN EZRA

However, the people were still unruly, for they had become Babylonian in their constitution. Therefore, there was the need for an Ezra, a priest who served God, and also a scribe, a scholar, who was skilled in the Word of God, skilled in the law of Moses (Ezra 7:6, 11). He bore the totality of the heavenly and divine constitution and culture. Ezra called the people together and confessed not only his own sin but also the sin of Israel, to bring them back to the Word of God.

THE RESPONSIBILITY OF THE ELDERS
TO TEACH THE SAINTS WITH THE TRUTHS

In the church life today, the main responsibility of the elders is to teach the saints with the truths. The Bible says that one of the qualifications of an elder is being apt to teach (1 Tim. 3:2). Paul tells us that certain elders may not have a job but may "labor in word and teaching" and therefore should be supported by the church (5:17-18). However, I have observed that some elders are deficient in the knowledge of the truth and may not even be clear whether a particular matter is an item of the truth.

Let me check with you about calling on the name of the Lord. Is calling on the name of the Lord a truth? No, it is not a truth. Calling on the Lord is necessary, and we need to have such a practice in our daily life, but calling on the Lord's name is not a truth. Likewise, baptism, presbytery, foot-washing, and pray-reading are not truths. On the other hand, justification by faith is a truth. Regeneration, sanctification, renewing, transformation, conformation, transfiguration, being made God in life and in nature but not in the Godhead—all these are truths.

Some elders may speak about life-practices such as calling on the Lord, pray-reading, praying without ceasing, not quenching the Spirit, and not despising prophesying, but they do not know how to teach the truths to the saints. For example, if these ones are asked about sanctification, they may be able to say only that to be sanctified is to be separated unto God. If they are asked about the difference between sanctification and renewing, they may not be able to explain the difference. Therefore, I say once again that all the elders need to know the truths and be able to teach the truths to others. All the elders need to spend much time to learn the truths. This is the duty, the responsibility, of an elder. Anyone who accepts an appointment to the eldership must fulfill this responsibility. Like Ezra, all the elders and co-workers must be skilled in the Word of God.

A GREAT FAMINE THROUGHOUT THE EARTH

Throughout the whole earth there is a great famine of God's Word. In Christianity today, both in Catholicism and in Protestantism, there is very little teaching of the truth. In many places, instead of the truth there are superstitions and pagan practices. For instance, in all of Latin America there is very little of the truth. I believe that this is the reason why our publications, which are full of the truth, are so well received there. In Latin America the people who love God also love our publications. These publications cover the entire Bible from the first page to the last.

THE NEED FOR EZRAS TO CONSTITUTE
THE PEOPLE WITH THE HEAVENLY TRUTHS

Both Brother Nee and I spent a great deal of time in learning to be skillful in the Word. Much of what we have learned has been put into print. We have almost completed the life-study of the Scriptures, and we have begun what we call the crystallization study. Today there is the need not just for Zerubbabels but for more Ezras. It would be unseemly for an elder to make decisions and expect the saints to follow them but not visit the saints with the truths. The real eldership is not to exercise authority. The real eldership is to visit the saints and to shepherd them, feed them, and take care of them by speaking to them concerning the truths. Today we need Ezras to teach the people, to educate them, and to constitute them with the heavenly truths.

TYPES OF THE RICHES OF CHRIST

I thank the Lord that, even though we are still so short in

many ways, He, for His own sake, has spread His recovery, with His riches, to more than two thousand cities throughout the earth. When the Israelites went back to Jerusalem, they were stirred up, they rose up, they went up, and they brought up 5,400 vessels of gold and silver (Ezra 1:7-11). These were the vessels which Nebuchadnezzar had brought out from Jerusalem and had put in the house of his gods. During the first return from the captivity, all these vessels were brought back to Jerusalem. Those vessels are types of the riches of Christ. After I came to this country, I released messages on the riches of Christ, and I also wrote a hymn on the unsearchable riches of Christ (*Hymns,* #542). In Ephesians 3:8 Paul speaks not only of Christ's riches but of Christ's unsearchable riches. Today the enjoyment of the riches of Christ is by His word.

THE LORD MOVING IN HIS RECOVERY BY HIS WORD

In His recovery the Lord is moving by His word, by the truth. His word is in the Bible, but the Bible needs the proper interpretation, which is found in the life-studies. If the co-workers and the elders study all our publications, there will be many Ezras in the Lord's recovery to constitute people with the heavenly truths.

LIFE-STUDY OF NEHEMIAH

MESSAGE ONE

AN INTRODUCTORY WORD
AND
THE REBUILDING OF THE WALL OF THE CITY
OF JERUSALEM UNDER NEHEMIAH

Scripture Reading: Neh. 1—7

With this message we begin the life-study of Nehemiah.

I. AN INTRODUCTORY WORD

A. The Book of Nehemiah
Being a History of the Rebuilding of the Wall
of the City of Jerusalem

The book of Ezra is a history of the return of Israel's
captivity and the rebuilding of the house of God as the ini-
tiation of God's recovery among His elect for His testimony on
the earth according to His economy. The book of Nehemiah is
a history of the rebuilding of the wall of the city of Jerusalem
as a continual recovery among His elect for His testimony for
the accomplishment of His economy.

B. The Writer

The writer of this book was Nehemiah, whose name means
"comfort of Jehovah." He was the cupbearer to the king
(1:11b). The whole book is a record of Nehemiah's trust in God
for his comfort in the trials and attacks of his enemies.

C. The Time

The contents of this book cover a period of about twelve
years, from 446-434 B.C.

D. The Contents

The contents of this book are the rebuilding of the wall of

the city of Jerusalem, which was destroyed by the enemies of Israel, and the further recovery of Israel's services and worship to God. In these messages I will use the word *constitution* to include the two matters of services and worship. The services plus worship equal constitution.

E. The Crucial Point

The crucial point of the book of Nehemiah is that the city of Jerusalem was a safeguard and protection for the house of God, which was in the city. This signifies that the house of God as His dwelling and home on the earth needs His kingdom to be established as a realm to safeguard His interest on the earth for His administration, to carry out His economy. The rebuilding of the house of God typifies God's recovery of the degraded church, and the rebuilding of the wall of the city of Jerusalem typifies God's recovery of His kingdom. God's building of His house and His building of His kingdom go together (Matt 16:18-19). The house of God on the earth needs His kingdom to safeguard the house and to carry out His eternal economy.

F. The Sections

The book of Nehemiah has two sections: the rebuilding of the wall of the city of Jerusalem under Nehemiah (chs. 1—7) and the reconstitution of the nation of God's elect (chs. 8—13).

II. THE REBUILDING OF THE WALL OF THE CITY OF JERUSALEM UNDER NEHEMIAH

A. The Report of the Condition of Jerusalem

In 1:1-3 we have a report of the condition of Jerusalem. According to this report the remnant of the returned captivity were in an exceedingly bad state and reproach (v. 3a). The wall of Jerusalem was broken down and its gates had been burned with fire (v. 3b).

B. Nehemiah's Prayer by Fasting

In his prayer by fasting (vv. 4-11), Nehemiah first praised God for what He is, praising Him for His keeping of His covenant and lovingkindness with those who love Him and keep His commandments (v. 5). Then he confessed the sins of the children of Israel (vv. 6-7) and asked God to remember His word to Moses that He would bring the captivity of His people even from the ends of heaven back to the place of His dwelling (vv. 8-9). Nehemiah stood on God's word and prayed according to it. Thus, God was bound by His own word. Nehemiah continued by begging God to hear his prayer and the prayer of those who took delight in fearing His name and to cause him to prosper and to find compassion before Artaxerxes the king of Persia (vv. 10-11a).

C. The King's Favor
in Giving Permission to Nehemiah

In 2:1-8 we see the king's favor in giving permission to Nehemiah.

D. Nehemiah's Journey to Jerusalem
and His Personal Observation

Verses 9 through 16 speak of Nehemiah's journey to Jerusalem and his personal observation of the condition of the wall of the city of Jerusalem. The leaders of the Moabites and Ammonites were greatly displeased about Nehemiah's seeking the good of the children of Israel (v. 10). The Moabites and the Ammonites, descendants of sons born of Lot, hated and despised the children of Israel.

E. The Rebuilding of the Wall of Jerusalem

Nehemiah 2:17-20 is a word concerning the rebuilding of the wall of Jerusalem. The leaders of the Moabites and Ammonites mocked and despised the children of Israel and asked whether they would rebel against the king by doing this (v. 19). Nehemiah answered them by saying, "The God of heaven Himself will make us prosper; therefore we His servants will rise up and build. But you have no portion nor right nor memorial in Jerusalem" (v. 20). This answer indicates that Nehemiah was very aggressive. He surely was not cowardly. Anyone who is cowardly cannot be a servant of God.

F. A Record of the Building of the Wall in Consecutive Sections

Chapter three is a record of the building of the wall in consecutive sections by all the children of Israel with the priests and Levites.

G. The Frustration of the Enemy

Chapter four describes the frustration of the enemy.

1. The Enemies Becoming Angry

The enemies became angry and greatly enraged, and again they mocked the Jews and despised their building (vv. 1-3).

2. Nehemiah Trusting in God

Nehemiah trusted in God by praying that God would return their reproach to themselves. Thus the Jews built the wall, and all the wall was joined together to half its height, for they had a heart to work (vv. 4-6). Today, no matter how much we may be mocked and despised, we should have a heart to build and should be aggressive.

3. The Enemies Being Angry Because the Building Work Was Advancing

The enemies were angry because the building work was advancing, and they conspired to come and fight against Jerusalem (vv. 7-8).

4. The Jews Praying to Their God and Setting a Watch against the Enemy

The Jews prayed to their God, and under Nehemiah's instruction and direction set a watch against the enemy day and night, ready to fight with weapons under the encouragement of Nehemiah, who instructed them to remember the great and awesome Lord and fight for their families. Half of Nehemiah's servants labored in the work, and half of them held weapons, ready to fight. Some built the wall and some carried burdens, taking the loads with one hand doing the work and with the other hand holding a weapon. The one who would sound the trumpet was beside Nehemiah, to gather them to fight, trusting that their God would fight for them. This indicates that, as the commander-in-chief, Nehemiah took the lead to watch. Thus, they labored and half of them held spears from the start of dawn until the stars came out, and Nehemiah and his brothers, servants, and the men of the guard, none of them took off their clothes. Each had his weapon at his right hand (vv. 9-23).

On the one hand, the children of Israel were prepared to fight; on the other hand, they trusted in God that He would fight for them. In this matter also they were aggressive. Those who are cowardly might say that, since God will fight for us, there is no need for us to do anything. But in a very real sense, God will help those who help themselves. If you do not help yourself, God will not help you. According to history, God does not help the cowardly. It is the aggressive ones who have received help from God.

H. The Settlement of the Interior Problem

Chapter five is concerned with the settlement of the interior problem. Often as we are fighting outwardly, we have an interior problem.

1. The People's Complaint

The people complained concerning the nobles' and rulers' imposing interest on them (vv. 1-5).

2. Nehemiah's Rebuke and Resolution

Verses 6 through 13 tell us about Nehemiah's rebuke and resolution. He set a great assembly against the nobles and rulers and told them that they did not walk in the fear of their God because of the reproach of the nations their enemies (vv. 7-9). They should have feared God because of the reproach and opposition from the nations.

Nehemiah, his brothers, and his servants had set an example by lending money and grain to others freely, and he charged the nobles and rulers to abandon such taking of interest (vv. 10-11). The nobles and rulers responded, saying that they would do what Nehemiah had said. Then Nehemiah called for the priests and took an oath from them with a solemn warning that God would shake out every man from his house and from his possessions who did not perform this promise (vv. 12-13a). The assembly said, "Amen," praising Jehovah, and acted according to their promise (v. 13b).

3. Nehemiah's Good Example

In verses 14 through 19 we see Nehemiah's good example.

a. Not Eating the Food Appointed for the Governor

Nehemiah and his brothers did not eat the food appointed for the governor for twelve years because of the fear of God (vv. 14-15).

b. Applying Himself to Work on the City Wall

Nehemiah applied himself to work on the city wall. He, his brothers, and all his servants, who were gathered there for the work, did not acquire fields. This means they did not receive any kind of payment. Rather, he fed richly at his table one hundred fifty Jews and rulers, besides those who came to him from the surrounding nations, not demanding the food appointed for the governor, for the building service was heavy on the people (vv. 16-18).

c. Asking God to Remember for Good All That He Had Done

Nehemiah asked God to remember for good all that he had done for the people (v. 19). He had the standing to ask God for this.

Here we should note that Nehemiah, as the governor, in the position of a king, was a man with a pure heart for the rebuilding of Jerusalem's wall in carrying out God's economy. He was not selfish, he did not seek his own interests, and he was not indulgent in sexual lust like all the kings, including David. Therefore, he was qualified to enjoy the top portion, the kingship of the good land promised by God to His elect. Instead of being self-seeking, he fed others for the purpose of building up the wall. In human history he might have been the only leader of a nation to behave in such a way. As a result, he was used by God.

I. The Further Frustration of the Enemy

Nehemiah 6:1-14 describes the further frustration of the enemy. First, they pretended compromise as part of a conspiracy to kill Nehemiah (vv. 1-4). They also slandered and threatened to weaken their hands from working, but Nehemiah prayed to God, saying, "Now strengthen my hands!" (vv. 5-9). Finally, the enemy acted by treachery with the false prophets and a false prophetess to cause Nehemiah to sin that they would have cause for an evil report in order to reproach him. However, Nehemiah prayed to God, asking Him to remember what they were doing (vv. 10-14).

J. The Completion of the Building

In 6:15—7:4 we have a record of the completion of the building. The building was completed on the twenty-fifth day of the month of Elul, in fifty-two days (6:15). All the enemies and all the surrounding nations were afraid and fell very low in their own eyes, knowing that this work was done with the help of God (v. 16). Verses 17-19 speak of the intimidation by Tobiah, who had relationships with the Jews in their intermarriage. In 7:1-4 Nehemiah gave his brother Hanani and the commander of the citadel charge over Jerusalem. Hanani was "a faithful man and feared God more than most" (v. 2). Lastly, God put it into Nehemiah's heart to enroll the returned captives by genealogy for the increase of the population of Jerusalem (vv. 5-73; cf. Ezra 2:1-70).

Nehemiah received help from God to carry out a great success in the work of rebuilding the wall of the city of Jerusalem. It is surely worthwhile for us today, especially the leading ones in the churches, to consider his example.

LIFE-STUDY OF NEHEMIAH

MESSAGE TWO

NEHEMIAH'S AGGRESSIVENESS

Scripture Reading: Neh. 1:1—2:8, 17-20

In this message we will consider Nehemiah's aggressiveness and the need for the proper aggressiveness in the Lord's recovery today.

THREE SECTIONS OF THE WORK
RELATED TO GOD'S HOUSE AND GOD'S KINGDOM

The books of Ezra and Nehemiah describe the return of the captives from Babylon to Jerusalem to rebuild the temple and repair the wall for God's house and God's kingdom. In order for God to have a house and a kingdom on the earth, three sections of work were needed. First, there was a need for some of the captivity to come back from Babylon to Jerusalem to lay a foundation for the formation of a nation. This required a strong government, a strong administration. Second, there was the need of teaching and education to bring the people of God into a culture that was according to God. Such a culture was not an Egyptian kind nor a Canaanite kind nor a Babylonian kind but was God's kind, a culture that expressed God. This kind of culture required a great deal of education. Third, there was the need to constitute the nation organically. This section of the work was concerned with the constitution of God's people.

The word *constitution* is ambiguous. According to the common notion, this word refers to a document which is the constitution of a country, for example, the Constitution of the United States of America. This understanding of constitution is too narrow. In our usage, the word constitution refers to something organic which has a number of elements. If the government of a country is constituted not only organizationally but also organically, that government will not be lifeless. On the contrary, such a government will be something that is living and organic.

The Leadership of Zerubbabel

At the expiration of the seventy years of the captivity in Babylon, the omnipotent, sovereign God moved in a hidden way to stir up King Cyrus openly to release the Israelite captives to go back to their own land to build up God's temple (Ezra 1:1-4). Also, King Cyrus brought out the vessels of the house of God, which Nebuchadnezzar had taken from Jerusalem and had put into the house of his gods (v. 7). These vessels were then returned to Jerusalem (v. 11). This return from captivity was under the kingly leadership of Zerubbabel, a descendant of the royal family of David (2:1-2). If we study carefully the record concerning him in the Bible, we will see that he was a strong governor and was very able in managing the people.

The Leadership of Ezra

Later, there was a second return from captivity under the priestly leadership of Ezra, a descendant of the priestly family. Ezra was not a high-ranking official in Persia. Rather, he was a priest and a scribe who was skilled in the law of Moses (7:6). Although he did not have any rank there in Persia, he was bold, strong, and aggressive in presenting a petition to the king of Persia. The king granted all his request, doing everything Ezra had asked.

The presenting of this petition was not initiated by God—it was initiated by Ezra. As the one who took the initiative in this matter, Ezra was a man who trusted in God and who was one with God. He was skilled in the Word of God and he knew God's heart, God's desire, and God's economy. Because of all this, he was a person of excellent character and reputation before the king. If Ezra had not had such a standing in the eyes of the king, the king would not have authorized him to appoint magistrates and judges (v. 25).

The Leadership of Nehemiah

Nehemiah, the son of Hacaliah, was not a counselor of the king nor a captain of the army. He was just a cupbearer, one who served wine to the king. But in his living and behavior he must have built up something that earned the king's respect. Nehemiah had never been sad in the king's presence (Neh. 2:1). One day the king said to him, "Why is your face sad, since you are not ill? This is nothing other than sadness of heart" (v. 2). Being aggressive, Nehemiah took advantage of this opportunity and said, "May the king live forever! Why should my face not be sad, when the city, the place of my fathers' graves, lies in waste and its gates are consumed with fire?" (v. 3). The king asked him what his request was, and Nehemiah asked the king to send him to Judah that he might rebuild the city of his fathers (v. 5). Nehemiah went on to request that letters would be given to him for the governors so that they would let him pass through. He asked also for a letter to Asaph, the keeper of the Park, so that he would give him timber (vv. 7-8). The king granted to Nehemiah all that he had requested.

THE AGGRESSIVENESS OF NEHEMIAH
IN VOLUNTEERING HIMSELF TO HIS BURDEN

We are not told that Nehemiah was stirred up by God. Rather, according to 1:1-2, he asked one of his brothers and some others who came from Judah about those who were left from the captivity and about Jerusalem. They told him that the people were in an exceedingly bad state and reproach and that the wall of Jerusalem was broken down and its gates had been burned with fire (v. 3). When Nehemiah heard this report, he wept, mourned, fasted, and prayed (v. 4). He did not call a prayer meeting, and he did not ask those who gave the report to pray about the situation. He prayed by himself with a real burden.

In principle, these three sections—government, education, and constitution—have been present in the Lord's recovery through the centuries. Some are raised up and stirred up by God, and some volunteer. Some are in a high position, and some are common people. But all must be bold and strong in character and aggressive. All who have been used by God through history have been aggressive persons. For example, both Paul and Martin Luther were very aggressive. Brother Nee also, even though he was a gentleman, was very aggressive.

Nehemiah surely was an aggressive person. He volunteered himself, in a sense, not to God but to his burden. He had a burden to rebuild the city of Jerusalem. His aggressiveness was very much used by God.

In the Lord's recovery today there are many good saints, but we are short of aggressiveness. If just five thousand among us were aggressive, the world would be turned upside down. If there were seven hundred aggressive ones in each continent, a great deal would issue forth for the carrying out of God's economy.

In our reading of the book of Nehemiah, we need to pay attention to Nehemiah's aggressiveness. Although he was a common man, a servant of the king, he was aggressive to volunteer himself to God and to his burden concerning the building up of the city. He was also aggressive in making his requests known to the king. When the king asked him about his sad face, he spoke to the king in a bold, aggressive way about his burden for the city of Jerusalem. It is important that we see this in the Word.

THE NATURAL VIRTUES AND CAPACITIES
BEING BROUGHT TO THE CROSS
IN ORDER TO BE BROUGHT INTO RESURRECTION

At this juncture we need to consider a matter that is significant in the typology in the Old Testament and in the fulfillment of the types in the New Testament. In typology many persons were temporarily used by God according to their natural capacity and natural virtues to signify something spiritual. An example of this is Nehemiah and his aggressiveness, which was a virtue in his human conduct. Whereas in typology natural things were used by God temporarily, in the fulfillment of the types in the New Testament, all the natural virtues and capacities should be brought to the cross. They need to be put to the cross and crossed out.

Many among us think that to put a certain thing to the cross means to put that thing to an end. In a sense, this is correct. However, according to the real significance of the cross of Christ, the cross does not mean merely that something is put to an end but that the natural things are crossed out in order to be brought into resurrection. The cross of Christ brings all natural things to death and burial. But according to the Bible, burial is followed by resurrection. Burial is therefore the threshold of resurrection. Whatever is buried will be resurrected. According to John 12:24 a grain of wheat falls into the ground, dies, and is buried. But this is not the end. After burial, something will come forth in resurrection.

The Example of Moses

Let us consider the example of Moses. I believe that Moses had a strong character and that in his natural constitution he was even more aggressive than Nehemiah was. At the age of forty Moses aggressively volunteered to save Israel out of the hand of Pharaoh, king of Egypt, but God came in to limit him, allowing him to fail and be disappointed. Moses was then "buried" in the wilderness for forty years. Eventually, the resurrecting God came in to resurrect Moses (Exo. 3:2-6).

The Example of Peter

God made us with certain virtues and capacities in our natural constitution. Matthew 25:15 tells us that the "talents" are given according to our "own ability," that is, our natural ability, which is constituted of God's creation and our learning. This ability needs to be crossed out and then brought into resurrection.

This was the experience of all the able and capable apostles, such as Paul and Peter. Peter, for instance, was in the "tomb" for three and a half years. Whenever he crept out of the tomb, the Lord Jesus would send him back to the tomb. On the night of the Lord's betrayal, Peter was so bold and aggressive as to say to the Lord, "Even if I must die with You, I will by no means deny You!" (Mark 14:31). Peter went on to tell Him that others might forsake Him but he would never do so. What boldness! What aggressiveness! The Lord told Peter, "Truly I say to you that today in this night, before a rooster crows twice, you will deny Me three times" (v. 30). Once again, Peter was put to the cross and buried.

Entering into Resurrection

If our natural capacity, natural ability, and natural virtues are not crossed out, they will cause a great deal of trouble and will be the source of big mistakes. But if we allow our natural capacity, ability, and virtues to be brought to the cross and die, we will be resurrected. Then in resurrection our capability, ability, and virtues will be many times greater than they were in the natural life. These things are still ours, but having passed through death and burial, they are now in resurrection. This means that we ourselves, with our capacity, ability, and virtues, have entered into resurrection. We continue to exist, but we with our natural ability have been brought into resurrection.

The reality of resurrection is the Spirit, and the Spirit is the consummated Triune God. Resurrection, therefore, is the consummated Triune God. Our natural capacity, ability, and virtue need to be transferred from our natural life into the consummated Triune God through death and burial. In ourselves we are natural, but when we are transferred out of ourselves into God, who is resurrection, we enter into resurrection.

An Important Principle

This is a very important principle for interpreting the types and their fulfillment. If we do not apply this principle, all the natural capacities, abilities, and virtues, unchecked by crucifixion, will be like "wild beasts" among us.

This has been the situation with many capable ones who came into the recovery and stayed for a while. They eventually realized that in the recovery there was no ground for them to employ their natural capacity and ability. Eventually, they left the recovery and formed a work for themselves. They were not willing to accept crucifixion and burial in order to be brought into resurrection. They could not take the cross. This is the reason certain capable persons who have come into the recovery do not remain.

God needs people who are highly educated. For example, he needed someone like Moses, who was "educated in all the wisdom of the Egyptians" (Acts 7:22). If Moses had not been an educated person, God would not have used him to give the law. However, we should not trust our natural wisdom or education. It is risky to put our trust in such things. We need to be one with God. If we are one with God, we will put our natural wisdom and education to the cross. The more we do this, the more we will be in resurrection.

It is never a loss to sow the "seed" of our natural ability into the ground. When we sow a seed we lose it temporarily, but eventually there will be a harvest in resurrection.

NEHEMIAH'S LIVING IN RESURRECTION

Nehemiah was one who lived not in his natural man but in resurrection. He was aggressive, but his aggressiveness was accompanied by other characteristics. First, he loved God. There is no doubt about this. He was born in captivity and was appointed to be the king's cupbearer, but he loved God. He also loved the holy land (signifying Christ), the holy temple (signifying the church), and the holy city (signifying the kingdom of God). He loved God and, in typology, he loved Christ, the church, and the kingdom. As a person who loved God, Nehemiah was one who contacted God. We are told a number of times that Nehemiah prayed to God (Neh. 1:4; 2:4b; 4:4-5, 9). Furthermore, Nehemiah trusted in God and even became one with God.

In himself Nehemiah's aggressiveness was natural, but in God his aggressiveness was in resurrection. Nehemiah was an aggressive person who loved God, the holy land, the holy temple, and the holy city, who contacted God and had fellowship with Him, who trusted in God, and who was one with God. As a result, he became the representative of God. We need to be clear about this in order to understand the intrinsic significance of the type according to the insight given by the Spirit.

LIFE-STUDY OF NEHEMIAH

MESSAGE THREE

THE RECONSTITUTION OF THE NATION OF GOD'S ELECT

(1)

Scripture Reading: Neh. 8—10

III. THE RECONSTITUTION OF THE NATION OF GOD'S ELECT

In this message we will begin to consider the reconstitution of the nation of God's elect (chs. 8—13).

A. Coming Back to God by Coming Back to His Law, His Word

In order to be reconstituted, we need to come back to God by coming back to His law, that is, His word (ch. 8). Suppose a fallen person wants to come back to God. If he would come back to God, he must come back to God's word. No one can come back to God without coming back to His word.

God's word reconstitutes us. We all have our own kind of disposition and habitual behavior, but God is able to reconstitute us through His word. This is why we need to read the Bible. God's word gradually changes our mind and our way of thinking. The word of God is one with the Spirit (Eph. 6:17). When the word of God works within us, the Spirit, through the word, spontaneously dispenses God's nature with God's element into our being. We may not even be aware that such a dispensing is taking place within us. By this way we are reconstituted.

Most of those who had returned to Jerusalem from the captivity in Babylon had been born not in Israel but in Babylon, and they were raised in Babylon. The Babylonian element had been wrought into them and constituted into their being. Therefore, after they returned to the land of their fathers to be citizens of the nation of Israel, they needed a reconstitution. Ezra was very useful at this point, for he was one through whom the people could be reconstituted with the word of God.

The constitution of a person provides the foundation for the constitution of a nation. A proper nation is not merely an organization but also a constitution. This is especially true of a nation's army. The army of the United States, for example, is constituted with many elements, and these elements afford the way for the individual soldiers to be reconstituted as parts of the army. Thus, the army is a constitution and not merely an organization.

God's intention with Israel was to have on earth a divinely constituted people to be His testimony. In order for God's people to be His testimony, they had to be reconstituted with the word of God. Under Ezra and Nehemiah the returned people of Israel were collectively constituted by and with God through His word to be a nation as God's testimony.

1. All the People of Israel Gathering as One Man and Telling Ezra to Bring the Book of the Law of Moses and Read to Them

According to Nehemiah 8:1-8 all the people of Israel gathered as one man before the Water Gate and told Ezra to bring the book of the law of Moses and read to them. Ezra did it and blessed Jehovah the great God, and all the people answered, "Amen, Amen," lifting up their hands; and they worshipped Jehovah with their faces to the ground. This indicates that rebellious Israel had been fully convinced and fully subdued by the word of God spoken through Moses.

The word of God is the solid base for the Spirit of God, who is God Himself, to dispense God's element into our being to cause us to be constituted with God. This should be our personal experience day by day. When we come together, we then need to read even more of the Word of God. To do this is to come together according to the way of the divine constitution.

In order to be reconstituted, we need to read the sixty-six books of the Bible again and again. As one who has been reading the Word for more than sixty-five years, I can testify that I have been reconstituted through the daily reading of the Word. Every day I am reconstituted a little more.

2. Nehemiah, Ezra, and the Levites Charging All the People to Sanctify That Day unto Jehovah Their God

Nehemiah the governor, Ezra the priest and scribe, and the Levites who helped the people understand charged all the people to sanctify that day unto Jehovah their God and not to mourn or weep, for all the people wept when they heard the words of the law. Nehemiah charged them to have a feast without grief, a feast full of joy. It was hard for the people to do this, because they had been convinced and subdued by the word to realize they were sinful (vv. 9-10a). Nehemiah said to them, "Do not be grieved, for the joy of Jehovah is your strength" (v. 10b). Then all "went their way to eat and to drink and to send portions and to make great rejoicing" (v. 12).

3. The Heads of the Fathers' Houses, the Priests, and the Levites Being Gathered to Ezra in order to Gain Insight into the Words of the Law

On the second day the heads of the fathers' houses, the priests, and the Levites were gathered to Ezra the scribe in order to gain insight into the words of the law (v. 13). Today many read the Bible without insight. Who has genuine insight into the word of the Bible? Here in verse 13 "insight" refers to the intrinsic significance. We all need to be helped to see the intrinsic significance of the word of the Bible.

Verses 14 through 18 tell us that they found in the law that Jehovah commanded the children of Israel to dwell in booths during the feast in the seventh month (the Feast of Tabernacles) and to publish and proclaim in all their cities and in Jerusalem to go out to the mountain and bring olive branches and other kinds of branches to make booths. All the assembly did it accordingly for seven days with great rejoicing, and day by day Ezra read in the book of the law of God. On the eighth day there was a solemn assembly, according to the ordinance. This indicates that they did everything according to the complete law, with the commandments, the statutes (the supplements to the commandments), and the ordinances (the judgments). They had a revival and became a new nation, constituted through and with the word.

B. Making a Clear Confession to God of Their Past and Making a Firm Covenant with God

In chapters nine and ten the people made a clear confession to God of their past and made a firm covenant with God.

1. The Descendants of Israel Separating Themselves from All Foreigners

The descendants of Israel separated themselves from all foreigners and stood, confessing their sins and the iniquities of their fathers and reading the book of the law of Jehovah (9:1-4).

2. Praising God as the Only God

They praised God as the only God, who created the heaven of heavens, the earth, and the seas with all that is in them, and who chose Abraham, brought him forth from Chaldea, and made a covenant with him to give him and his seed the land of Canaan (vv. 5-8). They knew God in this way and praised Him accordingly.

3. Enumerating All the Good That God Had Done for Their Forefathers

Next, they enumerated all the good that God had done for their forefathers, bringing them out of Egypt through the wilderness into the good land and giving them His law in spite of their arrogance and their stiffened neck and their refusing to listen to His commandments (vv. 9-25). What can deal with our arrogance, our stiffened neck, and our refusal to listen to God's commandments? Only the word of God can deal with these ugly things. The word of God can annul our arrogance. The word of God also can bend our stiff neck and cause us to listen to God's commandments.

4. Making a Further Confession of Their Disobedience and Rebellion

Following this, they made a further confession of their disobedience and rebellion (vv. 26-37). They confessed that, with a stiffened neck and a stubborn shoulder, they had cast God's law behind their back and had slain His prophets. Thus, they provoked God's wrath to give their good land to the oppression of the nations and give them, the people of Israel, into captivity to foreign lands. As a result, since the days of the kings of Assyria until that day, they had been in great distress.

5. Making a Firm Covenant in Writing

Because of all this they made a firm covenant in writing, and upon the sealed document were the names of their rulers, their Levites, and their priests (9:38—10:27).

6. The Rest of the People Entering into a Curse and an Oath

The rest of the people, the priests, the Levites, the gatekeepers, the singers, the temple servants, and all those who had separated themselves from the peoples of the lands unto the law of God entered into a curse and an oath (vv. 28-39). For them to enter into a curse meant that they would curse themselves if they did not keep the covenant. For them to enter into an oath meant that they could not cancel the covenant which they had made.

a. To Walk in the Law of God

In verses 29 through 31 we are told that they entered into a curse and an oath to walk in the law of God, which was given through Moses, and to keep and do all the commandments of Jehovah their Lord as well as His ordinances and statutes, not giving their daughters to the peoples of the land nor taking their daughters for their sons, keeping the Sabbath by not doing business, and foregoing the crops of the seventh year. To forego means to give up. According to God's ordination in His law, in the seventh year they were to give up sowing and reaping so that the land would have rest. Then the land would grow something by itself for the poor and the needy. This law concerning the seventh year reveals that God, the Lawgiver, is full of love, caring for the widows, the orphans, the needy ones, and the strangers.

The people agreed also to forego the exaction of every debt. They were not to force others to pay their debts. Therefore, in the seventh year they were not allowed to use the land, and they were not permitted to exact payment for every debt. The rich had to lend to the poor and then forego the exaction of the debt if the poor were unable to pay. For those who were unwilling to lend to the poor, God had many ways to balance the social wealth among the rich and the poor. In His wisdom and love God balances the wealth of His people. This matter also is related to the reconstitution of the nation of God's elect.

b. Laying upon Themselves Obligations to Offer Their Produce from the Land for Their Sacrifices

Furthermore, they laid upon themselves obligations to offer their produce from the land for their sacrifices to God and to provide for the service of the temple (vv. 32-39).

All these matters are items of the reconstitution of the people of Israel. The "wild" Israel was reconstituted with a divine constitution to be a separate, particular, sanctified people as a testimony of God on earth.

LIFE-STUDY OF NEHEMIAH

THE RECONSTITUTION OF THE NATION
OF GOD'S ELECT

(2)

Scripture Reading: Neh. 11—13

The books of Ezra and Nehemiah bear a strong intrinsic significance for the Lord's recovery today. We should not think that the Old Testament is unrelated to us. The Bible is written in two sections—the Old Testament and the New Testament. The first section contains pictures, while the second section contains the fulfillment of what is signified by the pictures. Without an intrinsic understanding of the Old Testament types, it is not easy to understand the fulfillment of God's economy in the New Testament.

In this message we will continue to consider the reconstitution of the nation of God's elect.

C. The Arrangement of
the Dwelling Place of the People
and the Appointment of the Officers
of the Levitical Service and of the Civil Affairs

The reconstitution of the nation of God's elect involved many aspects. In Nehemiah 11 we see that it involved the arrangement of the dwelling place of the people and the appointment of the officers of the Levitical service and of the civil affairs.

1. The Rulers of the People
Dwelling in Jerusalem

The rulers of the people dwelt in Jerusalem, the holy city, and the rest of the people cast lots in order to bring one in ten to dwell in Jerusalem. The people blessed all the men who offered themselves willingly to dwell in Jerusalem (vv. 1-2).

At that time it was a real burden for anyone to dwell in Jerusalem. Because of the constant threat of foreign invasion, not many were willing to live in Jerusalem. Therefore, there was the need of some arrangement by casting lots. Otherwise, there would not have been a sufficient number of people living in Jerusalem. The ones whose lot was to live in Jerusalem were required to move there. However, some were willing to volunteer to dwell in Jerusalem, and all the people blessed them. Today those who voluntarily go full time will be blessed by all.

2. A Record of the Arrangement and the Appointments

In verses 3 through 36 we have a detailed record of the arrangement and the appointments.

D. A Record of the Priests and Levites

Nehemiah 12:1-26 is a record of the priests and Levites. The main serving ones in the worship of God, which is the main thing in God's kingdom, were not the kings. The kings were not for worshipping God but for ruling the people. The main serving ones for the worshipping of God were the priests with the Levites, who were the servants of the priests.

1. Those Who Went Up with Zerubbabel and Joshua

In verses 1 through 21 we have a record of those faithful ones who went up from Babylon to Jerusalem with Zerubbabel and Joshua.

2. Those Who Served in the Days of Joiakim the Priest

Verses 22 through 26 are a record of those who served in the days of Joiakim the priest, of Nehemiah the governor, and of Ezra the priest, the scribe. They all were living in Jerusalem.

E. The Dedication of the Rebuilt Wall

The reconstitution also included the dedication of the rebuilt wall (vv. 27-43).

1. The People Seeking the Levites from All Their Places

The people sought the Levites from all their places, to bring them to Jerusalem in order to hold the dedication with rejoicing, thanksgiving, and singing with cymbals, harps, and lyres (vv. 27-29). The main service of the Levites was to sing in praise to God. For us today, singing hymns in the meetings is a primary need. Singing opens the heavens and brings us to the heavens. We should spend time to sing in different ways whenever we meet.

2. The Priests and the Levites Purifying Themselves

During the dedication the priests and the Levites purified themselves, and they also purified the people, the gates, and the wall (v. 30). Everything was purified, for they would not dedicate to God anything that was not pure.

3. Nehemiah Appointing Two Great Companies

Nehemiah appointed two great companies to give thanks to God, to go in procession, and to stand in the house of God with him (vv. 31-42).

4. The Offering of Great Sacrifices

They offered great sacrifices that day and rejoiced with their women and children, for God had caused them to rejoice greatly; and the joy of Jerusalem was heard from afar (v. 43). Today our neighbors should know that we are singing Christians, that we are the worshippers of God.

F. The Appointment of the Services of the Priests and the Levites and the Supply of Their Needs

The reconstitution also included the appointment of the services of the priests and the Levites and the supply of their needs (vv. 44-47). Nehemiah not only brought the serving Levites and priests into function; he also supplied their daily necessities. Before that time, no one had taken care of this matter properly.

G. The Clearance Exercised on Israel as God's Elect

Nehemiah 13:1-30a describes the clearance exercised on Israel as God's elect. There were many cleansings. This clearance was also part of the reconstitution of the nation of God's elect.

1. Separating All the Mixed Multitude from Israel according to the Law

First, all the mixed multitude were separated from Israel according to the law (vv. 1-3). When the people heard the law concerning Ammonites and Moabites not entering the assembly of God forever, they separated the mixed multitude from Israel.

2. Purifying the Chambers of the House of God

In verses 4 through 9 Nehemiah purified the chambers of the house of God from the evil occupancy by a relative of the priest who had been appointed over the chambers of the house of God. Eliashib the priest prepared for his relative Tobiah the Ammonite (2:10; 4:3; 6:1) a large chamber in the courts of the house of God where they had previously put the meal offering, the frankincense, and the vessels (13:5, 7). When Nehemiah perceived the evil that Eliashib had done for Tobiah, he was grieved and would not tolerate the situation. He cast all the household utensils of Tobiah out of the chamber and commanded that it be purified. Then Nehemiah returned to the chamber the vessels of the house of God, the meal offering, and the frankincense (vv. 8-9). In this matter there was a thorough clearance.

3. Removing the Negligence in Taking Care of the Need of the Levites

According to verses 10 through 13, Nehemiah went on to

remove the negligence in taking care of the need of the Levites. He found out that the portions of the Levites had not been given to them and he contended with the rulers regarding this. Then all Judah brought the tithe of the grain, the new wine, and the oil to the storehouses. Thus Nehemiah took care of all the daily necessities of the Levites.

4. Getting Rid of the People's Profaning of the Holy Sabbath

Nehemiah also got rid of the people's profaning of the holy Sabbath (vv. 15-22a). The Tyrians had been bringing their merchandise into Jerusalem and selling it there on the Sabbath. Nehemiah caused this profaning of the Sabbath to cease. He commanded that the gates of Jerusalem be shut before the Sabbath and not opened until after the Sabbath (v. 19). Then he commanded the Levites to purify themselves and keep the gates in order to sanctify the Sabbath day (v. 22a).

5. Cleansing the People and Especially the Priests from the Defilement of Their Marriages with the Nations

In verses 23 through 30a the people and especially the priests were cleansed from the defilement of their marriages with the nations. Nehemiah required those who married women of Ashdod, Ammon, and Moab to separate themselves from their foreign wives. In this matter he cleansed the people from everything foreign (v. 30a).

H. Appointing Duties for the Priests and the Levites, for the Wood Offering, and for the Firstfruits

Lastly, Nehemiah appointed duties for the priests and the Levites, for the wood offering at the appointed times, and for the firstfruits (vv. 30b-31a). All these arrangements were a reconstituting. Before Nehemiah's time the situation was a mess. The duties of the priests and the Levites were not clear, and there was not a proper arrangement for the wood offering and for the offering of the firstfruits of the produce of the land every year. There surely was the need for the reconstituting accomplished by Nehemiah.

In doing all these things Nehemiah asked God to remember him and spare him according to the greatness of His lovingkindness (13:14, 22b, 31b).

LIFE-STUDY OF NEHEMIAH

MESSAGE FIVE

THE LEADERSHIP OF NEHEMIAH FOR THE RECONSTITUTION OF THE NATION OF GOD'S ELECT

The leaders of the returned captivity were Zerubbabel of the royal family, Ezra of the priestly family, and Nehemiah of a common family. Among all the leaders in the history of Israel, these three were the top ones. Nehemiah was very common with no rank. There is no indication that his family had a high standing in society, and he did not have a high profession. Even though he served in the palace of the king of Persia, he was just a household servant.

Although Nehemiah was a common person without any position, he was placed in a very high position, a position which involved close contact with the king. Nehemiah was a cupbearer to the king (Neh. 1:11b). While wine was being set before the king, Nehemiah would take up the wine and give it to him (2:1a). Eventually, the king appointed this cupbearer to be the governor of Judah.

NEHEMIAH'S PARTICULAR CHARACTERISTICS

As one of the leaders of the returned captivity, Nehemiah had some particular and special characteristics.

Being a Pleasant Person with a Proper Attitude and Behavior

As a cupbearer to the king, Nehemiah must have been a person who was pleasant and sweet and who was always proper in his attitude and behavior. He was never sad in the king's presence (v. 1b). If Nehemiah had not been a pleasant person who fulfilled the king's requests, the king would not have allowed him to continue serving as a cupbearer.

A Person Who Loved God
and God's Interest on Earth

Nehemiah loved God, and he loved God's interest on earth concerning His economy. This interest included the good land, the temple, and the city of Jerusalem, all of which Nehemiah loved. Even though he was a common person without a rank such as that of a king or of a captain in the army, he took care of God's interest on earth.

One Who Prayed to Contact God in Fellowship

Nehemiah was also one who always prayed to God to contact God in fellowship. When he heard that the people in Jerusalem were suffering and that the wall of Jerusalem had been broken down and that its gates had been burned with fire, he wept, mourned, fasted, and prayed (1:2-4). In verse 11 he prayed, saying, "I beseech You, O Lord, let Your ear be attentive to the prayer of Your servant and to the prayer of Your servants, who take delight in fearing Your name; and cause Your servant to prosper today, and grant him to find compassion before this man." Here Nehemiah was praying that he would find favor with the king. When the king asked him regarding his request, Nehemiah "prayed to the God of heaven" (2:4).

A Person Who Trusted in God
and Who Was One with God

Furthermore, Nehemiah was a person who trusted in God and who was one with God. Burdens were placed upon his shoulder by God, but in bearing these burdens he trusted in God. Nehemiah knew that the good hand of God was upon him (vv. 8, 18), and he asked God to remember him (5:19; 13:14, 31). This indicates that he trusted in God and was one with God.

It was not easy for God to gain such a person as Nehemiah. In rank and profession he was very low, but he loved God and God's interest, he prayed for God's interest, contacting Him in fellowship, and he trusted in God and became one with Him. These are Nehemiah's particular characteristics in his relationship with God.

Altogether Unselfish

In his relationship with the people, Nehemiah was altogether unselfish. With him, there was no self-seeking. Even though he gained a high position as the governor of Judah—he was actually the acting king of Judah, representing the king of Persia—he never sought anything for himself. With Nehemiah there was no self-interest. He was always willing to sacrifice what he had for the people and for the nation. He was the governor, but he did not take any compensation for twelve years, because he realized that the building of the wall was a heavy burden on the people (5:14-18). He did not want to increase the burden on them. Instead of receiving compensation, he provided for the daily necessities of more than one hundred fifty men.

Nehemiah also was among those who were ready to fight against the enemy and he took part in the night watch (4:17-23). He did not leave these matters to others but participated in them himself.

Not Indulging in Lust

It is quite striking that there is no word concerning Nehemiah's marriage. I believe that, in contrast to the judges and the kings, Nehemiah had only one wife. He did not indulge in sexual lust. David and Solomon were both indulgent in this way. The indulgence in sexual lust was the main factor of the rottenness of David's family and the main factor behind the loss of the kingdom for David and his descendants. Nehemiah, however, was altogether different.

I believe that in the whole six thousand years of human history, there has never been such a one as Nehemiah. There were no complaints about Nehemiah from the people. Everyone appreciated him and was grateful for him. We may say that Nehemiah was an outstanding elder, the best example of what an elder should be. I hope that all the elders in the churches today will be like Nehemiah.

NEHEMIAH GOING TO EZRA FOR HELP
IN RECONSTITUTING THE NATION OF GOD'S ELECT

Nehemiah was a head, a ruler, of a nation, but he was altogether not ambitious. This is indicated by the fact that he recognized his need of Ezra. In reconstituting the nation, Nehemiah realized that he did not know God's Word. But Ezra, who was famous for his knowledge of the Word of God, was still alive, and Nehemiah was willing to go to Ezra for help. Many of today's leaders would not seek help in such a way. Instead, being ambitious, they would hold on to their position and not bring in an Ezra to help them. But because Nehemiah was not ambitious, he brought in Ezra. Nehemiah knew that without Ezra he could not reconstitute the people of God.

RE-EDUCATION FOR RECONSTITUTION

In order to reconstitute the people of God, there is the need to educate them with the word that comes out of the mouth of God, which expresses God. This means that to reconstitute the people of God is to educate them by putting them into the Word of God that they may be saturated with the Word.

The Israelites had been in Egypt for at least four hundred years. During those years they must have been constituted with Egyptian learning. Then they were brought to Babylon for seventy years. Zerubbabel, Ezra, and Nehemiah were all born and raised among the Babylonians. After the people of Israel returned from Babylon, they mixed themselves with the Canaanites. Thus, the Israelites were constituted with the Egyptian, Babylonian, and Canaanite culture. Nevertheless, they returned to be the testimony of God. But how could a people with a constitution of Egyptian, Babylonian, and Canaanite culture be God's testimony, the expression of the God-man? Such a people were not the God-men. How could they express God? In order to be the testimony of God, His expression, they needed to be re-educated in the Word of God.

THE RETURNED ISRAELITES
BECOMING GOD'S TESTIMONY

In addition to being re-educated, the people of Israel needed to be raised up in much the same way as parents raise their children. Parents not only educate their children but spontaneously and unconsciously impart themselves, nearly their whole being, into their children. Parents transfuse what they are and what they think into their children. Eventually, this constitutes their children to be the same as they are. This is what the children of Israel needed.

Before Nehemiah came back, the nation of Israel was a mess. The duties of the priests were not certain, and no one was taking care of the Levites and the serving ones. The singers were there, but no one had opened the way for them to sing and to be formed into companies. Nehemiah, with the help of Ezra, totally reconstituted the nation. Then Israel became a particular nation, a nation sanctified and separated unto God, expressing God. They were transfused with the thought of God, with the considerations of God, and with all that God is, making them God's reproduction. Everyone became God in life and in nature by this kind of divine constitution. As a result, they became a divine nation on earth expressing the divine character. They were reconstituted personally and corporately to be God's testimony. The returned captives became God's testimony through the reconstitution which took place under the leadership of Nehemiah.

The central and crucial point of the recovery books, which end with Nehemiah, is the matter of proper, adequate leadership. Whereas the record of the leadership in Judges, 1 and 2 Samuel, 1 and 2 Kings, and 1 and 2 Chronicles is dark, the record in Ezra and Nehemiah is bright. In Ezra and Nehemiah three leaders are mentioned: Zerubbabel, Ezra, and Nehemiah. They were all excellent leaders, but the best and the highest was Nehemiah. Nehemiah was the perfect leader, the best leader in human history. Only under the leadership of such persons as Zerubbabel, Ezra, and Nehemiah could Israel be reconstituted to be the testimony of God, the expression of God on earth, a people absolutely different from the Gentile nations. This is a type of what God wants the church to be today.

LIFE-STUDY OF ESTHER

MESSAGE ONE

AN INTRODUCTORY WORD
AND
THE SECRET CARE OF THE HIDING GOD
FOR HIS OPPRESSED ELECT IN THEIR DISPERSION

Scripture Reading: Esth. 1—2

With this message we begin the life-study of the book of Esther. Esther is a sweet book, covering, as its central subject, the secret care and the open salvation of the hiding God in Israel's captivity. God is omnipresent and also omnipotent, yet He is hiding. Nobody knows where He is.

The people of Israel had been scattered, dispersed, in their captivity. They probably told the Gentiles among whom they were living that their God was Jehovah. Gentiles, especially the rulers, might have said to the Israelites, "Where is your Jehovah? Is your Jehovah real and living? If He is, why are you here in captivity as slaves?" During the years of the captivity, God was hiding, and He is still hiding. Even today, in the church age, God is hiding Himself. Both for the children of Israel and for us today, it seems that there is no God in this universe. We need to realize that God is living and real, but He is hiding. He is a God who hides Himself (Isa. 45:15).

Because God's people became degraded and rotten, God disciplined and punished them by handing them over as slaves to the Gentile nations. Yet in His severity there is mercy (Rom. 11:22). While the people of Israel were in dispersion and captivity, God was taking care of them in a hidden way, and at the right time He came in openly to save them. Even when the captives of Israel were in the lowest situation, at the bottom, Christ was among them, suffering with them (Zech. 1:7-17).

On the one hand, God used the Gentile nations as tools to discipline His people. On the other hand, the hiding God was with the people of Israel, caring for them. Eventually, God used the Medo-Persian Empire to overthrow the Babylonian Empire. Cyrus, the king of Persia, was even called God's shepherd, one who would fulfill His desire (Isa. 44:28), and His anointed, one who would serve God's purpose (45:1-4). From this we see that the hiding God did many things for Israel in a secret way.

I. AN INTRODUCTORY WORD

Let us now consider some introductory matters.

A. The Writer

The writer of the book of Esther was most probably Mordecai (Esth. 9:20, 23). As Esther's cousin, he was the one who raised her.

B. The Time

The contents of this book cover a period of at least ten years during the reign of Ahasuerus (486-465 B.C.).

C. The Contents

The book of Esther gives us a vivid record of how the hiding God of Israel took care secretly of His oppressed elect in their dispersion and saved openly His persecuted elect in their captivity.

D. The Crucial Point

The crucial point of Esther is that the very God who chose Israel, the descendants of Abraham, as His elect, after He gave them into captivity to the Gentile nations, became a hidden God to them to take care of them secretly and save them openly in secrecy (Isa. 45:15). This is the reason that this book does not mention the name of God even at occasions when the name of God should be mentioned (Esth. 4:3, 16). Because this book shows us a hidden God, it does not mention the name of God.

E. The Sections

The book of Esther has two sections: (1) the secret care of the hiding God for His oppressed elect in their dispersion (chs. 1—2) and (2) the open salvation of the hiding God in secrecy to His persecuted elect in their captivity (chs. 3—10).

II. THE SECRET CARE OF THE HIDING GOD
FOR HIS OPPRESSED ELECT
IN THEIR DISPERSION AS SEEN IN ESTHER

Chapters one and two unveil the secret care of the hiding God for His oppressed elect as seen in Esther.

A. Establishing a Top King in the Gentile World

First, the hiding God established a top king in the Gentile world in prosperity, power, and glory over a great empire extending from India to Ethiopia (Africa)—1:1-2.

B. Causing the Top King to Depose His Queen because of Her Disobedience to His Word

Next, the hiding God caused the top king to depose his queen because of her disobedience to his word at his great banquet with his high officials (vv. 3-22). The king commanded that the queen come before him wearing the royal crown in order that he might present her to those attending the banquet. However, the queen refused to come at the king's command. As a result of her disobedience the queen was deposed, and the position of queen became vacant.

C. Raising Up a Jewish Orphan Virgin to Be Crowned by the Top King as His Queen

Finally, in His secret care the hiding God raised up Esther, a Jewish orphan virgin, to be crowned by the top king as his queen (2:1-18). Esther saved the king from being assassinated, telling the king in Mordecai's name of those who planned to assassinate him (vv. 19-23).

Our God is omnipresent, omnipotent, merciful, and full of forgiveness. Although He is such a God, He is also the hiding God. Because our God is a hiding God, others may check with us and ask, "Where is your God? Where is His kingdom?"

When we are questioned in such a manner, we may want to answer in this way: "My God is hidden. I cannot see Him, and you cannot see Him either. But you need to realize that sooner or later my hidden God will come in to do something on my behalf and to deal with those who do not believe in Him."

I can testify concerning this from my experience. More than forty-five years ago, I, along with several other co-workers, was arrested and imprisoned by a small Chinese army that betrayed China and worked for the Japanese military police. The entire Christian community in that city was shocked, because they knew that we could very easily be executed like other Chinese who had fallen into the hands of the Japanese invading army. We did not know what to expect, but the hiding God intervened in a wonderful way using a particular person as an Esther.

The wife of the captain of the Chinese army under the Japanese military police had been the wife of a schoolmate of mine who had died of tuberculosis. When he was dying, his wife asked me to visit him, and I did so and had an intimate conversation with him. He eventually died, and some time later she remarried. After I was arrested and imprisoned, a medical doctor who was meeting both with us and with other Christians heard about my situation. He then went to speak to the woman who had married the captain of that Chinese army. The two were close friends, and the doctor who was meeting with us told the woman that I and several others had been imprisoned and that she should ask her husband to release us. She spoke to her husband about us that very day. He loved her and was willing to fulfill her request.

That night he appeared to judge our case. We were taken from our cells and stood before him to be judged. I was the first one to be examined by him. He looked at me, asked me my name, and told me that everything was all right and that I was free to go home peacefully. He said the same thing to the others who had been arrested with me. At the time none of us knew what had taken place behind the scene. Later I realized that, in His secret wisdom, the hiding God had prepared an Esther for us. He had raised up a Chinese widow to become the wife of the man who would judge our case. Just as the king of Persia listened to Esther and did what she said out of his love for her, so this man listened to his wife and released us from prison. This surely was due to the care of the hiding God.

Today we need to realize that the omnipotent God whom we are serving is still hiding Himself, especially when He is helping us. We cannot see Him, and apparently He is not doing anything for us. Actually, He is with us all the time and, in a hidden way, He is doing many things for us.

LIFE-STUDY OF ESTHER

MESSAGE TWO

THE OPEN SALVATION
OF THE HIDING GOD IN SECRECY
TO HIS PERSECUTED ELECT IN THEIR CAPTIVITY

Scripture Reading: Esth. 3—10

In this message we will cover chapters three through ten.

III. THE OPEN SALVATION
OF THE HIDING GOD IN SECRECY
TO HIS PERSECUTED ELECT IN THEIR CAPTIVITY
AS SEEN IN MORDECAI

These chapters are concerned with the open salvation of
the hiding God in secrecy to His persecuted elect in their
captivity as seen in Mordecai.

A. Haman's Plot
to Destroy All the Jews in Medo-Persia

In chapter three we see Haman's plot to destroy all the
Jews in Medo-Persia.

1. An Agagite by the Name of Haman
Being Promoted to the Highest Seat
above All the Princes Who Were with the King

The Agagites were enemies of God. God charged Saul to
slay all the Agagites, but he failed to do this and thereby
offended God.

An Agagite by the name of Haman was promoted (no
doubt at the instigation of Satan, the adversary of God) to
the highest seat above all the princes who were with the king.
The king commanded all his servants to bow down and pay
homage to Haman, but Mordecai did not bow down or
pay homage because of his Jewish belief in the unique God

(vv. 1-4). He believed in one God and refused to bow down to anyone other than God.

2. Haman Being Filled with Rage and Plotting Not Only to Kill Mordecai but Also to Destroy All the Jews throughout the Empire

Haman was filled with rage and plotted not only to kill Mordecai, the one who refused to pay him homage, but also to destroy all the Jews throughout the empire. He had the king send a decree to each province of his empire to destroy all the Jews, both young and old, children and women, in one day, the thirteenth day of the twelfth month, and to plunder their spoil (vv. 5-15). Haman's evil intention was to destroy all the Jews and to take away their wealth.

B. Mordecai's Confrontation of Haman's Plot through Esther's Close and Intimate Contact with the King

In 4:1 through 8:2 we have an account of Mordecai's confrontation of Haman's plot through Esther's close and intimate contact with the king.

1. All the Jews and Esther Fasting

When all the Jews and Esther heard of what Haman intended to do and learned that the king had even issued a decree to carry out Haman's intention, they fasted (4:3, 16). Although they fasted for their supplication to God, contrary to what we would expect, in verse 16 there is no mention of the name of God. While Esther and all the Jews were fasting, Haman, under the plot with his wife and friends, made a gallows on which to hang Mordecai (5:9-14).

2. The King Being Unable to Sleep and Finding the Report of How Mordecai Had Saved Him

The king could not sleep, so he gave orders to have the book of the records of the chronicles brought, and they were read before him (6:1). The king found in the records the report of how Mordecai had saved him from being assassinated by two of his eunuchs, and he decided to bestow honor and dignity on Mordecai. While the king was considering this, Haman came into the court to ask the king about hanging Mordecai (vv. 2-6). The king was thinking about honoring Mordecai, and Haman was thinking about hanging him. When the king asked Haman what should be done for the man whom the king desires to honor, Haman answered, "Let a royal robe be brought, one which the king has worn, and a horse on which the king has ridden and on whose head a royal crown has been set. And let the robe and the horse be delivered into the hand of one of the king's most noble princes; and let them array the man whom the king desires to honor and make him ride on horseback through the street of the city; and let them proclaim before him, Thus shall it be done for the man whom the king desires to honor" (vv. 8-9). At this juncture, the king commanded Haman to put on Mordecai a royal robe which the king had worn, make Mordecai ride through the street of the city on a horse on which the king had ridden, and proclaim before Mordecai, "Thus shall it be done for the man whom the king desires to honor" (vv. 10-11). After Haman did this, he hurried to his house, mourning and with his head covered (v. 12).

3. Esther Pointing Out to the King That Haman Was the Wicked Adversary and Enemy Who Conspired to Kill All the Jews

At her feast with the king and Haman, Esther the queen pointed out that Haman was the wicked adversary and enemy who conspired to kill all the Jews. The king immediately sentenced Haman to death and commanded his men to hang Haman on the gallows which he had prepared for Mordecai. On that day the king gave the house of Haman, the enemy of the Jews, to Esther the queen and took off his signet ring, which he had taken from Haman, and gave it to Mordecai, making him the second man to the king in the whole empire (7:1—8:2).

C. The Open, Triumphant Victory of the Jews over Their Enemies

In 8:3 through 10:3 we see the open, triumphant victory of

the Jews over their enemies—the open salvation of their hiding God to rescue them from their persecutors.

1. The King Issuing a Decree
through Mordecai

The king issued through Mordecai a decree to authorize the Jews to destroy all their enemies throughout his empire from India to Ethiopia, one hundred twenty-seven provinces (8:3-14).

2. The Jews Having
Light, Gladness, Joy, and Honor

Mordecai went forth from the presence of the king in royal robes of blue and white and with a large crown of gold and a garment of fine linen and purple. The city of Susa the capital shouted and rejoiced, and the Jews had light, gladness, joy, and honor. Throughout every province and every city, wherever the king's decree came, the Jews had gladness, joy, a feast, and a good day. Many from among the peoples of the land (the heathen) became Jews, for the fear of the Jews had fallen on them (vv. 15-17).

3. The Jews Destroying
All Their Enemies throughout the Empire

The Jews destroyed all their enemies throughout the empire under the reign of King Ahasuerus in the influence of Esther the queen with Mordecai as the second to the king (9:1-16). All the princes of the provinces, the satraps, the governors, and those who did the king's business helped the Jews because of the fear of Mordecai, who was great in the king's house and whose fame went forth throughout all the provinces and who became greater and greater (vv. 1-4). In Susa the capital in two days the Jews destroyed eight hundred of their enemies and they hanged Haman's ten sons upon the gallows (vv. 5-15). In the provinces the Jews assembled and destroyed seventy-five thousand of those who hated them, thus having rest from their enemies (v. 16).

4. The Triumphant Jews
Appointing and Establishing the Days of Purim

The triumphant Jews appointed and established the four-teenth and fifteenth days of the month Adar as the Purim to celebrate their triumphant victory over their enemies (vv. 17-32). In this way the feast of Purim was established among the Jews for the remembrance and celebration of the two days during which they destroyed their enemies through-out the great empire of Persia. These days were to be days of feasting and rejoicing and of sending portions to one another and gifts to the poor (vv. 17-19, 22). These days were to be remembered and kept throughout every generation, every family, every province, and every city, and the remembrance of them was not to fade from their seed (vv. 26-28). The appointment and the establishment of the Purim was con-firmed by Queen Esther and Mordecai the Jew in writing with all authority (vv. 29-32).

5. Mordecai Becoming Second to King Ahasuerus and Great among the Jews

Mordecai became second to King Ahasuerus and great among the Jews and well-regarded by the multitude of his brothers, one who sought the good of his people and who spoke for the welfare of all his seed, that is, all the children of Israel (10:1-3).

IV. A CONCLUDING WORD

A. A Crucial Hidden Point

The story of the book of Esther is a crucial hidden point for the fulfillment of God's calling to Abraham for a land, a seed (a people), and the blessing to all the nations (Gen. 12:1-3; 22:17-18).

B. For the Fulfillment of the Promise through Moses

The story of this book is also for the fulfillment of the promise through Moses that after God gave Israel into captivity, He would still take care of them (Deut. 4:27-31).

C. For the Fulfillment of the Prayer of Solomon

In addition, the story of the book of Esther is for the fulfillment of the prayer of Solomon on the day of the dedication of the temple that God would take care of His elect in their captivity (1 Kings 8:46-53).

D. For the Keeping of the Lineage of the Genealogy of Christ

Moreover, the story recorded in the book of Esther is also for the keeping of the lineage of the genealogy of Christ through the survival of Israel in their captivity that Christ might be brought into the human race. If all the Jews had been destroyed, there would have been no lineage of Christ's genealogy for Christ to be brought into humanity.

E. To Keep a People for the Possessing of the Holy Land for the Coming Kingdom of Christ

Finally, the story of the book of Esther is to keep a people for the possessing of the holy land for the coming kingdom of Christ. The people of God's elect who returned from captivity were small in number, yet they occupied and possessed at least a small portion of the earth, the holy land. This was significant because the earth had been usurped by Satan, and there seemed to be nothing left for the God of heaven and earth. However, God brought back a small number of His people to possess the holy land as a base for Christ to come back to establish His kingdom on earth.

THE ESCHATOLOGY OF THE CHURCH
ACCORDING TO THE DIVINE REVELATION
OF THE SCRIPTURES

Scripture Reading: Rev. 17:1-6, 16; 14:8; Matt. 13:37-42; 1 Cor. 3:9b-15; Rev. 21:1-11, 18-21

We need to see that there is not only an eschatology of the world, the study of the end of the world situation, but also an eschatology of the church. Our study of this crucial matter is according to the divine revelation of the Scriptures. We believers in Christ are not only in the world but also in the church. The genuine church exists within Christianity. Christianity has become very great and includes mainly the Catholic Church and the Protestant church. The Catholic Church and the Protestant church were not there at the time of the apostle Paul. What was there at his time was the original and recovered church. The recovered church refers to the original church. These two are one.

Paul rebuked the Corinthian believers in his first Epistle to them by telling them that they were trying to divide Christ. There were various parties in Corinth who were saying, "I am of Paul," "I am of Apollos," and "I am of Cephas." The self-supposed "spiritual" ones said, "I am of Christ" (1:12-13a). Thus, there were four divisions in Corinth. The church in Corinth was an original church, but it had degraded; it had lost something. At that juncture Paul wrote them. His Epistles to them were recovery books; they recovered the church in Corinth.

By reading Paul's second Epistle to Timothy, we can also see that at Paul's time the church had degraded. Some had left the Christian faith. Others, like Alexander the coppersmith, opposed Paul to the uttermost (4:14). But Paul himself declared that he had kept the faith (v. 7). Second Timothy is a book of recovery. The original church existed only for about half a century. The apostles established the original church within less than fifty years. But while Peter, John, and Paul were still living, the church fell from its original state to a degraded state, a deformed state, and even a transmuted state. This is why the Epistles were written. All the "second" letters of Peter, John, and Paul (e.g., 2 Peter, 2 and 3 John, 2 Corinthians, etc.) were letters of recovery. All these letters were for recovering the lost church.

At John's time, some even said that Christ never came in the flesh (1 John 4:2-3; 2 John 7). Others said that Christ was not the Son of God but eventually became the Son of God (1 John 2:22-23). The church had become deformed, changed in form, and transmuted, changed in nature. Thus, John wrote to the believers to recover them. At the time of the apostles we can see the original and recovered church.

The recovered church came into being just a little later than the original church. The original church lasted only for a short time. It was born into a sick situation, an unhealthy environment. When the apostle Paul was sent by the Holy Spirit from Antioch to Asia to preach the gospel and to set up churches, the opposing Jews came to frustrate him. After the churches were established, the Gnostics came in to make trouble. Thus, the church became sick either from Judaism or Gnosticism. The original church did not last too long, but God would not let the church be lost without any kind of recovery. This is why the Lord as the Head of the Body charged the apostles Peter, John, and Paul to write their later Epistles to recover the church. We have to realize that the Lord's recovery began at the end of the first century. In every century afterward, the Lord raised up a number of "Ezras" and "Nehemiahs" to recover, to reconstitute, the church.

In the first five centuries, there was only the original and recovered church. Then near the end of the sixth century the Catholic Church came into existence. At that time the pope was recognized as the authority of the Catholic Church. The Protestant church came into existence at the time of Martin Luther during the Reformation in the sixteenth century. Today there are still these three kinds of churches.

The church of the recovery is always taking a narrow way. All of those who participate in the recovered church learn the special lessons in the Christian life. They learn to know Christ, to know themselves, and to know the flesh. They learn how to be crucified to live the God-man life. All the members of the church should be God-men because the church is formed with the deified man. The high truth of God becoming a man that man might become God in life and nature but not in the Godhead was discovered by the church fathers in the second century. This was something of the Lord's recovery. With us the Lord's recovery began in mainland China seventy-two years ago. Today there are mainly three kinds of churches on earth: the Catholic Church, the Protestant church, and the original and recovered church. We must choose the original and recovered church because it is genuine.

THE REAL CONDITION AND END
OF THE CATHOLIC CHURCH

The real condition and end of the Catholic Church are clearly unveiled in Revelation 17. The first six verses tell us the condition, and the last three verses tell us the end. The condition is illustrated in a figure of speech by a golden cup (v. 4). A cup signifies something that is presented to a person for him to drink to meet his need. The golden cup signifies that in outward appearance the apostate church does have something of God. The Catholic Church believes that Christ is God, that He was born of a virgin, and that He died for the sins of sinners and resurrected. In their recent catechism, they also pointed out that God became a man that man might become God. In today's Protestant churches, on the other hand, there are modernists who do not believe that Christ is God, that He was born of a virgin, and that He died on the cross as the Redeemer. They consider that Christ was a martyr and do not believe that He resurrected.

In Revelation 17 the Roman Catholic Church is called "MYSTERY, BABYLON THE GREAT" (v. 5). There are even some Catholic scholars who have recognized that the Great Babylon in Revelation 17 refers to the Catholic Church. In Matthew 13 the Lord likened the Roman Catholic Church to a woman who took leaven and put it into fine flour (v. 33). Most fundamental expositors of the Bible say that the fine flour refers to Christ as food to both God and man. Leaven signifies evil things (1 Cor. 5:6, 8) and evil doctrines (Matt. 16:6, 11-12). It includes all evil things such as heresy, idolatry, and adultery. Thus, the Catholic Church is a mixture.

The cup which the woman has in her hand is golden, but it is full of abominations and the unclean things of her fornication (Rev. 17:4). In figure, gold signifies the divine nature of God. Hence, the apostate church does have something of God, but she is full of evil things such as heresies, idolatry, pagan practices, spiritual fornication, and even physical fornication. For a woman to practice fornication means that she has many husbands. The church should be married to Christ and to the truth of the Bible. Not only is Christ the Husband, but also the truth, the Word of God, is the Husband. The Word of God and Christ are one. The Catholic Church has accepted Christ and the Word of God, yet it has also received many heresies and idols. This has made her a spiritual fornicator.

The Catholic cathedrals are full of idols. G. H. Pember pointed out that one of the saints in the Roman Catholic Church is actually Buddha (see the *Life-study of Revelation,* Message 51, p. 585). In Manila there is a statue of a so-called Jesus at the entrance of a certain cathedral. The feet of this statue have been touched and even kissed by people so many times that there is a hole there. This is idolatry, but it is in a "golden cup."

One young person from a Catholic family received the Lord Jesus and then went to his parents to tell them that he had the Lord Jesus in him. His parents responded by saying that they already had Jesus, and they pointed to a picture of the so-called Jesus hanging on the wall. Because they had such a picture, they thought they had Jesus.

In 1937 when I was traveling in the interior of China, a case of demon possession was brought to my attention. I said that in principle either sin or some idols or images in that woman's home would give the ground for demon possession. Eventually, I learned that on her wall was a picture of the so-called Jesus, and I told her to burn it. From the moment she burned that picture, the demon departed. The Catholic Church is full of idols, heresy, and all kinds of pagan and heathen practices. This is the real condition of today's Catholic Church.

Revelation 17 also tells us the end of the Catholic Church. At the end of this age, the Antichrist will make a covenant with the Jews for seven years. In the middle part of this seven-year period, he will break this covenant (Dan. 9:27) and exalt "himself above all that is called God or an object of worship" (2 Thes. 2:4). He will persecute all religions, and the first religion persecuted by him will be that of the Catholic Church. This is because both Antichrist and the Catholic Church will be centered in Rome. Revelation 17:16 says, "And the ten horns which you saw and the beast, these will hate the harlot and will make her desolate and naked and will eat her flesh and burn her utterly with fire." This means that Antichrist and his ten kings will persecute the Great Babylon and burn her. That will be the end of the Catholic Church.

THE GENERAL CONDITION AND END
OF THE PROTESTANT CHURCH

The Protestant church is full of false believers (Matt. 13:37-42). In Matthew 13 the Lord told us that the kingdom of the heavens is like a man who sowed good seed of wheat in his field, but his enemy then came and sowed tares in the midst of the wheat. His slaves then asked if they should go to collect these tares. But the man's response was, "Let both grow together until the harvest, and at the time of the harvest I will say to the reapers, Collect first the tares and bind them into bundles to burn them up, but the wheat gather into my barn" (v. 30). The Lord said that at the consummation of this age, He will send His angels to collect all these tares, signifying all the false, nominal Christians in any kind of church, and will cast them into the lake of fire (vv. 40-42). They will be thrown directly into the lake of fire, having no need to pass through the formality of any judgment. Their end will be the same as Antichrist and the false prophet. Both of them will also be thrown into the lake of fire directly, without any formal judgment (Rev. 19:20).

THE GENUINE CONDITION AND END
OF THE ORIGINAL AND RECOVERED CHURCH

The original and recovered church is the genuine church. The church in Corinth was a genuine church. Paul told them, "You are God's cultivated land, God's building" (1 Cor. 3:9). He was telling them that they were the genuine believers, the real ones who had received the Lord Jesus, who had been regenerated, and who were going to be sanctified, renewed, transformed, conformed, and glorified. On the one hand, they were God's farm to grow Christ. On the other hand, they had to be transformed from plant life to minerals. They had to grow so that they could be transformed to become gold, silver, and precious stones, the material for God's building. Paul laid the unique foundation of Christ, but the believers' progress would depend upon how they grew and how they built upon this foundation. If they built with wood, grass, and stubble, these materials would be burned (vv. 10-13).

At His coming back, the Lord will judge and deal with not only the Catholic Church and the Protestant church but also the original and recovered church. He will summon all His genuine believers in any kind of church to His judgment seat (2 Cor. 5:10; Rom. 14:10; 1 Cor. 4:5) to be judged and dealt with by Him. In that judgment He will discern whether they have built with gold, silver, and precious stones or with wood, grass, and stubble. The work of wood, grass, and stubble will be consumed, and those who have worked with these worthless materials "will be saved, yet so as through fire" (1 Cor. 3:15). On the other hand, those who have built with gold, silver, and precious stones will be the materials for the constitution of the New Jerusalem in the millennium and be consummated in the New Jerusalem in the new heaven and new earth.

At the Lord's coming back, the overcomers who are transformed into gold, silver, and precious stones will be awarded to be in the New Jerusalem in the thousand years of the kingdom. Revelation shows us that the New Jerusalem will be the

Paradise of God in the thousand years for the overcomers (2:7). But those who produce wood, grass, and stubble will have their work burned at the Lord's coming back, and they will be saved as through fire. They will be disciplined by the Lord for one thousand years. Eventually, through the Lord's patience, they will be perfected and transformed also into precious material for God's building. At the end of the thousand years, they will also join and participate in the New Jerusalem in its consummation. This is the genuine condition and end of the original and recovered church.

Today we have a choice as to which way we will take. Will we take the Catholic way, the Protestant way, or the original and recovered way? If we take the original and recovered way, how will we take it? Will we take it in a condition of idleness? Revelation shows us that among all the genuine believers, only those who are like Paul in struggling to pursue Christ will gain and enjoy Christ. They will be the overcomers. We may be in the original and recovered church, but what kind of condition are we in? Are we endeavoring to be the overcomers to close this age? In other words, are we endeavoring to live a God-man life with ourselves and our flesh always being crucified on the cross that we may live by His divine life to express Christ? If so, we will be able to proclaim, "For to me to live is Christ. I live to magnify Christ whether through life or death by the bountiful supply of the Spirit of Jesus Christ."

We should be such overcomers who are living and magnifying Christ day by day. We should be constituted as those who pursue Christ at any cost, always forgetting the past and going forward to gain Christ. To gain Christ actually means to live and magnify Christ. We can live and magnify Christ by living a crucified life toward ourselves, our flesh, our natural life, and everything other than Christ. We are crucified in every way to live Christ by the bountiful supply of the Spirit of Jesus Christ. Then we not only live Him but also magnify Him. How much we gain Him depends upon how much we magnify Him. This is the living of the God-men, who are the overcomers.

We should not say in a light way that we are God-men. This is not a light matter. We may praise the Lord for the highest peak of the divine revelation that God has become a man that man may become God in life and in nature but not in the Godhead. But we should say, "Lord, I need Your mercy. I need Your abounding grace. Otherwise, how could I become God in life and in nature? Every day I need to live a crucified life to gain Christ, to magnify Christ."

THE NEW JERUSALEM
AS THE ULTIMATE CONSUMMATION
OF GOD'S ETERNAL INTENTION

Eventually, we will be in the ultimate consummation of God's purpose, the New Jerusalem (Rev. 21:1-11). The New Jerusalem is constituted with three kinds of materials: gold, pearl, and precious stones (vv. 18-21). Gold signifies God in His divine nature, pearl signifies the redeeming and regenerating Christ, and precious stones signify the transforming Spirit. This is the consummated Divine Trinity constituting Himself into our being to make us gold, pearl, and precious stones that He may have an enlargement for His eternal expression, the New Jerusalem.

About the Author

Witness Lee was born in 1905 in northern China and raised in a Christian family. At age 19 he was fully captured for Christ and immediately consecrated himself to preach the gospel for the rest of his life. Early in his service, he met Watchman Nee, a renowned preacher, teacher, and writer. Witness Lee labored together with Watchman Nee under his direction. In 1934 Watchman Nee entrusted Witness Lee with the responsibility for his publication operation, called the Shanghai Gospel Bookroom.

Prior to the Communist takeover in 1949, Witness Lee was sent by Watchman Nee and his other co-workers to Taiwan to ensure that the things delivered to them by the Lord would not be lost. Watchman Nee instructed Witness Lee to continue the former's publishing operation abroad as the Taiwan Gospel Bookroom, which has been publicly recognized as the publisher of Watchman Nee's works outside China. Witness Lee's work in Taiwan manifested the Lord's abundant blessing. From a mere 350 believers, newly fled from the mainland, the churches in Taiwan grew to 20,000 in five years.

In 1962 Witness Lee felt led of the Lord to come to the United States, and he began to minister in Los Angeles. During his 35 years of service in the U.S., he ministered in weekly meetings and weekend conferences, delivering several thousand spoken messages. Much of his speaking has since been published as over 400 titles. Many of these have been translated into over fourteen languages. He gave his last public conference in February 1997 at the age of 91.

He leaves behind a prolific presentation of the truth in the Bible. His major work, *Life-study of the Bible,* comprises over 25,000 pages of commentary on every book of the Bible from the perspective of the believers' enjoyment and experience of God's divine life in Christ through the Holy Spirit. Witness Lee was the chief editor of a new translation of the New Testament into Chinese called the Recovery Version and directed the translation of the same into English. The Recovery Version also appears in a number of other languages. He provided an extensive body of footnotes, outlines, and spiritual cross references. A radio broadcast of his messages can be heard on Christian radio stations in the United States. In 1965 Witness Lee founded Living Stream Ministry, a non-profit corporation, located in Anaheim, California, which officially presents his and Watchman Nee's ministry.

Witness Lee's ministry emphasizes the experience of Christ as life and the practical oneness of the believers as the Body of Christ. Stressing the importance of attending to both these matters, he led the churches under his care to grow in Christian life and function. He was unbending in his conviction that God's goal is not narrow sectarianism but the Body of Christ. In time, believers began to meet simply as the church in their localities in response to this conviction. In recent years a number of new churches have been raised up in Russia and in many European countries.

OTHER BOOKS PUBLISHED BY
Living Stream Ministry

Titles by Witness Lee:

Abraham—Called by God	978-0-7363-0359-0
The Experience of Life	978-0-87083-417-2
The Knowledge of Life	978-0-87083-419-6
The Tree of Life	978-0-87083-300-7
The Economy of God	978-0-87083-415-8
The Divine Economy	978-0-87083-268-0
God's New Testament Economy	978-0-87083-199-7
The World Situation and God's Move	978-0-87083-092-1
Christ vs. Religion	978-0-87083-010-5
The All-inclusive Christ	978-0-87083-020-4
Gospel Outlines	978-0-87083-039-6
Character	978-0-87083-322-9
The Secret of Experiencing Christ	978-0-87083-227-7
The Life and Way for the Practice of the Church Life	978-0-87083-785-2
The Basic Revelation in the Holy Scriptures	978-0-87083-105-8
The Crucial Revelation of Life in the Scriptures	978-0-87083-372-4
The Spirit with Our Spirit	978-0-87083-798-2
Christ as the Reality	978-0-87083-047-1
The Central Line of the Divine Revelation	978-0-87083-960-3
The Full Knowledge of the Word of God	978-0-87083-289-5
Watchman Nee—A Seer of the Divine Revelation ...	978-0-87083-625-1

Titles by Watchman Nee:

How to Study the Bible	978-0-7363-0407-8
God's Overcomers	978-0-7363-0433-7
The New Covenant	978-0-7363-0088-9
The Spiritual Man • 3 volumes	978-0-7363-0269-2
Authority and Submission	978-0-7363-0185-5
The Overcoming Life	978-1-57593-817-2
The Glorious Church	978-0-87083-745-6
The Prayer Ministry of the Church	978-0-87083-860-6
The Breaking of the Outer Man and the Release ...	978-1-57593-955-1
The Mystery of Christ	978-1-57593-954-4
The God of Abraham, Isaac, and Jacob	978-0-87083-932-0
The Song of Songs	978-0-87083-872-9
The Gospel of God • 2 volumes	978-1-57593-953-7
The Normal Christian Church Life	978-0-87083-027-3
The Character of the Lord's Worker	978-1-57593-322-1
The Normal Christian Faith	978-0-87083-748-7
Watchman Nee's Testimony	978-0-87083-051-8

Available at
Christian bookstores, or contact Living Stream Ministry
2431 W. La Palma Ave. • Anaheim, CA 92801
1-800-549-5164 • www.livingstream.com